10134

W9-BLN-293

IMAGINING HITLER

IMAGINING
HITLER

ALVIN H. ROSENFELD

INDIANA UNIVERSITY PRESS   BLOOMINGTON

Manufactured in the United States of America

Library of Congress Cataloging in Publication Data

Rosenfeld, Alvin H. (Alvin Hirsch), 1938–
Imagining Hitler.

Bibliography: p.
Includes index.
1. American literature—20th century—History and
criticism.   2. Hitler, Adolf, 1889–1945, in fiction,
drama, poetry, etc.   3. Hitler, Adolf, 1889–1945—
Influence.   4. English literature—20th century—
History and criticism.   5. World War, 1939–1945—
Literature and the war.   6. National socialism in
literature.   7. Holocaust, Jewish (1939–1945), in
literature.   I. Title.
PS228.H58R6   1985   810'.9'358   84-48456

ISBN 0-253-13960-0

1 2 3 4 5 89 88 87 86 85

FOR ERNA, GAVRIEL, AND
DALIA

One and a half generations after his death in the bunker, Hitler
was like the little man upon the stair in the old song.
He wasn't there, but he wouldn't go away.

—CORDON CRAIG

Contents

Contents

VI.
Hitler, Jews, and Justice
79

VII.
Pop Culture, Politics, and the Iniquity of Images
103

ACKNOWLEDGMENTS

A number of friends and colleagues read portions of this work in earlier manuscript drafts. While they bear no responsibility for whatever flaws the book may still have, I am certain it is better for the criticisms they were generous enough to offer me. I wish to thank Matei Calinescu, Todd Endelman, Michael Rosenblum, Scott Sanders, and Colleen Stamos. Robert Waite helped me straighten out a problem in the sources relating to Hitler's early years in Vienna, and I wish to publicly acknowledge my debt to him. Yoel Kaminsky was resourceful in helping me track down numerous books and articles used throughout this study. And Patsy Ek was, as always, cheerful, diligent, and efficient in typing; I am grateful to her for all of her good work.

I wish to thank the National Endowment for the Humanities for awarding me a Research Fellowship and the Office of Research and Graduate Development at Indiana University, under the direction of Dean Morton Lowengrub, for a Research Leave Supplement. Such support allowed me to take leave of my teaching duties during 1983–84, the period when I most needed time off to finish writing this book.

Earlier versions of some of these chapters appeared in *Salmagundi, Dissent, Midstream,* and the Simon Wiesenthal Center *Annual,* and I thank the editors for permission to reprint.

INTRODUCTION

This is not a book about Hitler but about the ghost of Hitler. It is an attempt to chart the course of an evolving myth, one that has its origins in the political history of Europe of half a century ago and is today enjoying a thriving afterlife within the imagination of much of the Western world. While I look especially to the popular forms of imagination, and mostly to fiction, to locate the sources of this myth, this is not a book of literary criticism in the conventional sense. Rather, it is an attempt to traverse a wide body of literature in order to get at certain strains of the demonic that find their reflection in writing but aspire to a more than literary life. It is, in other words, a book about culture, or about the death of culture, as symbolized by a figure who, more than any other, stands for the deformation and ultimately the defeat of all our cultural ideals.

Forty years after Hitler's death, what is it that accounts for the continuing Nazi hold on the imagination, a hold that seems to be not just lingering but in some ways increasing or intensifying? Why does Hitler preoccupy us so, and in shapes that are overwhelmingly fictive or fantastical and not predominantly historical? What does he symbolize today, and how do these symbolizations square with what we know about the man and the destructive events he brought on?

This is not the place to sketch in a biography of Adolf Hitler, but it might be apposite, by way of illustrating the point of these questions, to set beside what we assume to be common knowledge of the main lines of Hitler's life and career the following excerpt from a recent fiction:

> Adolf Hitler was born in Austria on April 20, 1889. As a young man he migrated to Germany and served in the German army during the Great War. After the war, he dabbled briefly in radical politics in Munich before finally emigrating to New York in 1919. While learning English,

he eked out a precarious existence as a sidewalk artist and occasional translator in New York's bohemian haven, Greenwich Village. After several years of this freewheeling life, he began to pick up odd jobs as a magazine and comic illustrator. He did his first interior illustration for the science-fiction magazine *Amazing* in 1930. By 1932, he was a regular illustrator for the science-fiction magazines, and, by 1935, he had enough confidence in his English to make his debut as a science-fiction writer. He devoted the rest of his life to the science-fiction genre as a writer, illustrator, and fanzine editor. Although best known to present-day SF fans for his novels and stories, Hitler was a popular illustrator during the Golden Age of the thirties, edited several anthologies, wrote lively reviews, and published a popular fanzine, *Storm*, for nearly ten years.

He won a posthumous Hugo at the 1955 World Science-Fiction Convention for *Lord of the Swastika*, which was completed just before his death in 1953. For many years, he had been a popular figure at SF conventions, widely known in science-fiction fandom as a wit and non-stop raconteur. Ever since the book's publication, the colorful costumes he created in *Lord of the Swastika* have been favorite themes at convention masquerades. Hitler died in 1953, but the stories and novels he left behind remain as a legacy to all science-fiction enthusiasts.

This little "biography" is taken from the Author's Page of *Lord of the Swastika*, which purports to be a science fiction novel by Adolf Hitler, as presented by Norman Spinrad in *The Iron Dream*. Undoubtedly written as a satire, this fictionalization of Hitler nonetheless serves to drive home the point that the history of Nazism, as exemplified by innumerable fanciful portraits of its central figure, has become so plastic to the contemporary imagination as to be almost whatever one would like it to be. As the chapters that follow show, it is not that Nazism has been altogether denuded of its aspect of terror (although sometimes it has) but that its aura of destructive power has been turned into sexual and political fantasies, religious allegories, pseudohistories, science fictions. Nazism, in other words, has been lifted from its historical base and transmuted into forms of entertainment and political bad faith. What a generation ago stood before us as a historical and moral scandal of unprecedented proportions is today a source of lighthearted amusement, popular distraction, pornographic indulgence, and antisemitic slander.

This book attempts to chart the course of this devolution and to offer at least partial explanations for it. The genesis of the problem is taken up in chapter 1, which describes the "survival myth" and begins to speculate on the implications of keeping Hitler alive through various kinds of frauds and fictions. The most recent of these frauds—the so-called "Hitler Diaries"—is presented as only the latest and most notorious example of numerous attempts over the years to develop an image of Hitler that would fascinate or otherwise appeal to the popular mind. Chapter 2, devoted as it is mostly to the work of Hugh Trevor-Roper, examines the tension between history writing and cultural myth-making and shows how even the most devoted opponents of Nazism are at times drawn to elaborate aspects of the Nazi mystique in their writings, whose intention is expressly to deprive that mystique of any lingering power. This chapter thus begins a series of reflections on strains of contention between fiction and historical consciousness that continues through the remainder of the book. Chapter 3 takes up some prominent examples of realistic fiction and, through close examination of the work of Ernst Weiss, Beryl Bainbridge, and Richard Hughes, argues that the historical novel, even when well done, fails to offer credible or compelling reconstructions of Hitler and his times.

Realism is left behind for the most part in chapter 4, which shifts attention to works of fantasy and, in particular, to the eroticization of Nazism, a widespread and especially pernicious development that exploits antifeminine as well as antisemitic feeling. Thrillers, spy novels, pornographic fictions, and other forms of pulp literature comprise the central focus of the first part of this chapter, while the second part is given over to an examination of D. M. Thomas's *The White Hotel*, a recent highbrow novel that draws upon many of the same conventions as the more popular, lowbrow writings. Chapter 5 continues the discussion of *The White Hotel* in terms that link this novel to some of the writings of William Styron (*Sophie's Choice*) and Mary McCarthy (her commentary on *Eichmann in Jerusalem*) and the impulse to "transcend" or otherwise to deny the reality of Hitler's Holocaust of the Jews. In chapter 6, which is devoted wholly to an examination of George Steiner's *The Portage to San Cristóbal of A.H.*, the discussion turns to questions of justice, both legal and aesthetic, and the increasingly determined attempt to Judaize Hitler and to equate Nazism with Zionism. These themes are examined in their furthest extension to date in chapter 7, which describes the accelerating tendency within popular culture to circulate and otherwise to revive and sell images of Hitler, and the concurrent political dangers of seeing recent events through a screen of metaphors appropriated from the rhetoric of the Third Reich.

In sum, this is a book about the imagination of Nazism as manifested in popular representations of the Nazi Führer. Readers who wish to learn about cinematic treatments will be disappointed, for I devote myself almost exclusively to literature and touch on films only in passing (such readers can consult the work of Kracauer, Sontag, Friedländer, Insdorf, and others). While the phenomenon I set out to describe is now pervasive through much of the Western world (as it is through parts of South America and the Middle East), I have chosen to confine myself almost entirely to developments within this country. Nevertheless, the popular images of Hitler that I elaborate upon are hardly localized to the United States, and those interested in analogous developments elsewhere should have no trouble extrapolating from the examples and analyses offered here.

In doing so, I strongly suspect they will arrive at many of the same conclusions established in this book. They will see, for instance, that, despite our growing distance in time from the end of World War II, Hitler remains a figure of preoccupying concern and is steadily evolving not only through fiction but *as* a fiction. They will see as well that such fictions both exalt the image of Hitler by casting it in terms that intrigue and excite the imagination and neutralize it by making the man seem so ordinary. These transformations appear, it is worth noting, in all the media of cultural expression and can be the product of high art and high scholarship as well as of hack writing and the more commercial strains of cinematic and television production. It is a common feature of current representations of Hitler, in fact, to project an enhanced image of the man, even when there may be no conscious or deliberate intention to do so. To linger over him at all in word or in image is almost inevitably to augment the current fascination with Nazism, fascination that is relentlessly unhistorical and hence an easy trigger for fantasies of the most extreme kind.

Fiction's role in the awakening of these desires has its root, I suspect, in some deep-seated aversion to sustaining a realistic sense of gross historical pain while at the same time paying an almost promiscuous kind of attention to acts of human suffering and distress. Within literature and the other arts, there is a long-standing interest in evil and injustice, but otherwise the popular mind does not seem prepared to recognize the extent of mass atrocity within our midst and is inclined to withhold an unconditional acknowledgment of the tragic side of human existence. To be sure, most people "know" about the murderous excesses of Nazism—vaguely, partially, and usually in broad and imprecise outline—but few want to take upon themselves the burden of living with a consciousness transformed by the anguish, guilt, and pain that necessarily accompany a fuller awareness of Hitler's crimes.

A partial awareness, however, can be a stimulus to the myth-making predilections of popular imagination, following which it becomes easy to reshape even the cruelest of events into configurations of altered memory and reawakened desire. All art is transforming, and thus inherently in conflict with the testimonial or documentary ideals of history writing (practice, as we know, is something else). As every writer is aware (sometimes uneasily, more often not), it is only when the fact dies that the fiction has a chance to be born, a truth expressed with uncommon candor not long ago by the British novelist Anthony Burgess:

> When I took up, twenty-eight years ago, the novelist's career, I became aware that this entailed the abandonment of any dormant inclinations to scholarship that I possessed. Fiction is a lying craft and it has no pretensions to exact knowledge. . . . Nothing could be less scholarly than the average novel, even when its basis is historical fact. . . . The novelist is a confidence trickster, while it is the task of the scholar to teach skepticism.

Because I admire what Mr. Burgess says here and align myself with his notion about the proper task of scholars, I have proceeded in this book in a way that may not please all of my readers. An avid reader of fiction, I am at the same time skeptical of and in continuous debate with fiction's infidelity to history. Moreover, I am, unfashionably, a critic of a certain moral bent, distrustful of confidence tricksters, and thus am likely to be an opponent as often as a devotee of "the lying craft." Particularly with regard to the history that lies behind my concerns in this book—a history still far from being broadly acknowledged let alone fully assimilated, a history in some quarters actively and maliciously under siege—I am far more likely to side with those who give precedence to the claims of factuality than I am with those who claim priority for fiction. While not favoring a prose colored by preachment, I could not write this book oblivious to what I take to be the stakes involved in the attenuation and distortion of historical memory. Lucy Dawidowicz formulates a significant part of my concerns (but surely not just *my* concerns) when she writes, in an essay on "Smut and Anti-Semitism," that

> today a sizable population views the Third Reich's terrors and murders only through a prism of pornography. Their loss of moral affect becomes a loss of political affect. Morally dulled, they become more vulnerable to the appeal of antihumanist movements and eventually more receptive to the obscenity of anti-Semitism.

Antisemitism is always intolerable, and in the shadow of Hitler, in which we still live our anxious lives, altogether inadmissible. Yet this is not a book about the threat of a new antisemitism so much as it is a descriptive account and analysis of the old menace in its new reflections. What is uncanny about the new fascination with Hitler is its resemblance—often recognizable in impulse, idiom, tone, and direction—to the fascination of the 1930s and 1940s. The jackboots are not about to pound the pavements, but something disturbingly familiar is pounding again in the heads of too many people, heads that are being filled with popular images of the Third Reich of the kind described throughout this book. The release of these images across all the media of culture does not in and of itself mean an instant return to bad times, but it does suggest a rapid removal of the fear of those bad times and of the moral disgrace that once attended them. In writing about this phenomenon, therefore, I have not pretended to affect a dispassionate or disinterested style but have allowed myself to exercise a liberal degree of pointed criticism whenever warranted. If validation for this mode of discourse is needed, I find it in the admonitory words of Jean Améry:

> It is true that moral indignation cannot hold its ground against the silently erosive and transformative effects of time. It is hopeless, even if not entirely unjustified, to demand that National Socialism be felt as an outrage with the same emotional intensity as in the years immediately following the Second World War. No doubt, there exists something like historical entropy: the historical "heat gradient" disappears. . . . But we should not foster this entropy; on the contrary, we should resist it with all our power. . . . Reality is reasonable only so long as it is moral.

Introduction

Given the nature of the subject brought under scrutiny in these chapters, writing needs to be moral, too, lest it appear to reinforce the very phenomenon it sets out to contend with. The challenge in writing about popular imaginings of Hitler, therefore, is to expose the disease without becoming infected by it, a challenge I hope I have met more often than not in the pages of this book.

A second challenge, this one theoretical and methodological, derives from the kinds of material I have chosen to study and my ways of studying them. The reader will find an unusual mix of cultural expression here—pulp and smut mingling with novels of high seriousness, the ephemera of popular culture set side by side with efforts at developing more permanent forms of art. The intention is neither to elevate the former nor to reduce the latter but, by bringing them into association, to reveal some widely shared patterns of imaginative response to the Nazi mystique. A broad-based elaboration of what Saul Friedländer has recently called a "new discourse" on Nazism is now underway and is evident in the academy as well as in the street. While recognizing the distinctions that need to be maintained between these very separate realms, I have sought to locate within each of them manifestations of a yielding to those peculiar fantasies of criminality and corruption originally generated by Nazism and incarnated in the figure of Adolf Hitler.

In pursuit of this Hitler, my primary aims have been not so much to probe ideological intentions or to render aesthetic judgments (although at times I have done both) but to trace an association of recurrent images across several different levels of culture. In traversing these levels, which in this book means in going from *schlock* to respectable intellectual discourse and back again, I am fully aware of differences in literary kind, intention, and value and recognize that each appeals to its own kind of audience and solicits its own response. All, however, seem drawn by those regnant symbols of evil and extremity that Hitler more than anyone else provoked and that fictions of him continue to sustain.

In examining these fictions, I have encountered a problem that remains unresolved. In a literary-critical sense, it is a problem of representation, but beyond that it is a deeper moral and epistemological problem and forces one to ponder what mind and imagination are capable and desirous of knowing about historical evil. To state the problem in its simplest terms: at least on the evidence of the literature that has been given us to date, no representations of Hitler, highbrow or low, seem able adequately to present the man or satisfactorily to explain him. Those works that demonize him distort through tropological excess, making him into a creature altogether unlike any to be found in humankind, whereas those works that normalize him tend to minimize his wickedness and diminish or deny his destructive side. Between these contrasting images of the demonic and the domestic figure, the "real" Hitler, one feels, somehow gets lost or slips away.

I do not pretend to have recovered him in this book. What I have done, or at least have sought to do, is to point up some of the consequences of what is at one and the same time an imaginative obsession and an imaginative failure. Hitler, one comes to understand, simultaneously haunts and defies the contemporary imagination, which, with respect to the whole Nazi past, seems drawn between a willed forgetfulness and a kind of mythologizing memory. As a consequence, the ghost of Hitler has been set free from the strictures of historical consciousness and enjoys a second life through art.

To trace the course of his latter-day wanderings and to reflect upon the cultural implications of his reappearance among us is the whole purpose of this book. If, in reading it, there are those who are brought to newly assess what they expect from history and what they will tolerate from fiction, then this descent into some of the darker regions of imaginative possession will have been worth the taking.

IMAGINING HITLER

I

The Return of the Führer

Ideas too far-fetched for fiction can
yet be swallowed hook-line-and-sinker
when offered as fact.

—RICHARD HUGHES

"HITLER IS ALIVE." The headline, printed in bold, black letters, is meant to startle and to frighten. For a moment, it may do both. At
the least, it amazes. The caption underneath is no less breathtaking: "AT
AGE 93, NAZI MADMAN MASTERMINDED ARGENTINA'S INVASION OF THE
FALKLANDS." Whose eyes could possibly turn away from news like that?

The story that follows tells how Hitler faked his widely publicized
suicide in 1945, managed to get out of Berlin and into South America, and
has been living ("lurking") ever since in a Buenos Aires suburb, from
where he has been "gathering his forces and waiting for the right moment
to launch his fiendish plans." The spring of 1982 seems to have been that
moment, for, according to the *National Examiner*, the tabloid that featured this story in its July 6 number of that year, Hitler not only per-
suaded the Argentine colonels to seize the Falklands but also arranged for
the shooting of Israel's ambassador in London, thus touching off two wars
at once. The idea was to foment chaos enough to frighten the world and
throw it into massive confusion. Amid this turmoil the Führer would
emerge once more in a final push for world domination.

There are lots of pictures to illustrate this story—one of Hitler at the
height of his power, right arm outstretched in rigid salute; another, an
artist's drawing, depicting how Hitler would look today (not at all bad for
93); still another of a sharp-eyed American psychic gripping an ornate

Nazi dagger; then one of Israeli Nazi-hunter Tuwia Friedman holding up some snapshots of Mengele (also traced to Argentina and said to be Hitler's personal doctor there); and finally a map of North and South America dominated by a huge swastika.

The swastika is obligatory, as is the presence of an Israeli sleuth, the gleaming dagger, and the many exclamation points that hype the story. We are, after all, reading of Hitler in the *National Examiner*.

But if it weren't the *Examiner* it would be the *Police Gazette*, which periodically brings us up-to-date on Hitler's latest doings; or the *National Lampoon*, one of whose recent issues featured a collection of "Hitler's Favorite Cartoons"; or the *New York Times*, which a while back ran an article on the sale at auction of an object alleged to be Hitler's skull; or still another television docudrama on Hitler or one of his henchmen; or a new game, or T-shirt, or rock record, or pendant, or puzzle.

Hitler has not gone without a good deal of posthumous attention, in other words. Go to the movies and you will see him. Look at the popular bookracks and you can't miss him. There is a growth industry in Hitler picture books, biographies, films, fiction, other assorted memorabilia, tokens, and trinkets that symbolize the Nazi period and hold it steadily before us. As one of his biographers recently put it, "more will be written about Adolf Hitler than about anyone else in history with the exception of Jesus Christ."

What explains this fascination with Hitler and keeps memory of the man alive? And to what degree is it not memory at all but imagination gone a little wild, propelled by mythologizing impulses when not simply manipulated by the profit-making motives of popular culture? One needs to linger awhile over these questions, for the reality that gives rise to them seems to have a good deal of energy behind it and is not likely to go away soon. If anything, we may be only at the beginning of the marketing of Adolf Hitler, with the future bullish on a revival of interest in the man and the myth.

Certain things can be said right off, for by now they are recognizable as part of literary convention. The bad omens and sensational frights that go with the bold headlines announcing the latest sighting of Hitler are generic. As with any piece of formulaic fiction, one expects them and probably would miss them if they were not there. The formulas have an interesting history of their own. They derive from a survival myth that began to develop as far back as the spring of 1945, owing at least in part to a fascination with the phenomenon of the empty tomb. Thus, while we are as sure as we possibly can be that Hitler committed suicide in his underground bunker in Berlin, the body itself was never recovered, at least not by us. Russian troops, and not American or British forces, first reached the part of the city where Hitler was holding out, and just what teeth and bones they carried back with them to the Kremlin remains to this day in dispute. The matter was responsibly, even masterfully studied by Hugh Trevor-Roper in the months immediately following the end of the war, but despite the historian's best efforts, and they were considerable, the impulse to hold open a "mystery" surrounding Hitler's last days, and periodically to exploit it in fanciful ways, remains alive. The result has been a kind of willed confusion, itself the product of capricious and sensationalizing journalism, political calculation, and the exploitation of the most primitive layers of folk belief. One sees it on all sides.

Thus, while the Russians controlled whatever evidence there was from the start, Stalin said one thing about the Führer's remains, some of his generals another. Eisenhower seems to have been a bit befuddled about the facts of Hitler's end and did not quite know what to say. As for the Germans, they swung between theories of the most contradictory sort, at times admitting he was dead, at times helping to sustain a new Barbarossa myth. There were notions that Hitler had flown away from his beleaguered bunker at the last moment and was in hiding somewhere, possibly in Germany but more likely in South America or Antarctica or even, in a more exotic version of his survival, in a monastery high in the Himalayan mountains of Tibet.

To his credit, and also a little bit to his dismay, Trevor-Roper foresaw the development of such stories at the very time he was writing a book intended to put them to rest. "The facts are now clear," he wrote, "and if myths, like the truth, depend on evidence, we are safe." Yet myths do not depend on evidence, at least not of the historical sort, but on feelings that are a good deal harder to contain, and in the face of their clamorings it is not easy to ensure our safety. As Trevor-Roper put it, "Reason is powerless against the obstinate love of fiction." That is especially the case when the fictions mimic or otherwise appeal to the power of religious language. Years after the Führer's death, for instance, a Nazi group in England was still proclaiming that "Adolf Hitler, like Jesus Christ, could

· 3 ·

never die. Hitler was the reincarnated Spirit of Christ, at the Second Coming." However outrageous this simile will appear to believing Christians, the fact is that from the time of Hitler's ascent to power until today it has been a constant one, confirming the view that a prominent motive behind the rise and retention of the Hitler myth is a quasi-religious one. It is no doubt for this reason that the same mass market magazines that like to showcase stories on Hitler's survival devote periodic attention to stories about the afterlife of Elvis, the shroud of Turin, and psychic conversations with the dead. The same number of the *National Examiner* that proclaimed Hitler to be still alive, it is worth noting, also carried a story announcing two miraculous appearances of the Virgin Mary. While the first story may be a cruel parody of the second, each depends upon the suspension of the rational faculties and a loosening of the demands for historical verification. Closely allied to "the obstinate love of fiction," in other words, is common gullibility, which is easily appealed to and even more easily exploited by the crafty.

As soon as one talks about the crafty, one begins to deliberate upon the art of fiction, which is literary craft at its most elaborately developed and, so we like to believe, most purposeful. Yet it is difficult to find much serious purpose in most of the imaginative literature about Hitler that has been published over the years. I refer to a wide assortment of longer and shorter fiction that runs the gamut from science fiction to sword and sorcery religious and political allegories, from pornographic revivals of the darkest sides of Nazi cruelty to South American spy thrillers. There are also periodic literary attempts to normalize Hitler, or to de-mythologize him, to show him to be a regular guy, more or less like you or me. We have had the raging Hitler, the contrite Hitler, the artistic Hitler, the tender Hitler. And we have had repeated attempts to bring him to trial, attempts which usually end up portraying him as much in the role of the defiant accuser as the guilty accused.

Hitler, in other words, has become a kind of silly putty in the hands of postwar fictioneers, who stretch him this way and that, devising as many shapes from his memory as the motive for metaphor will allow. A short list of pertinent titles illustrates the protean side of his postwar life-in-literature: there is *Young Adolf* and "Darling Adolf," *Hitler's Wife* and *Hitler's Daughter*, "Swastika" and *Lord of the Swastika*, *A God for Tomorrow* and *Twilight of the Gods*, "Hitler Meets Haman" and "Pharaoh Meets

Hitler," *The Man Who Killed Hitler* and *The Death of the Führer, The Day of Reckoning* and *If Judgment Comes.*

This list can be considerably extended, but it already carries us from childhood to the grave. There are also several novels that guarantee him a life beyond the grave through experiments with cloning. And there are any number of fictions that trace his posthumous wanderings here and there—"His Last Battle" situates him in a small Peruvian town, "The Wandering Gentile" sees him on America's west coast, while "With Hitler in New York" carries him east. As our writers have tended to dream him up, he is likely to be found almost anywhere, almost any time, and in the shape of almost anybody. So long, that is, as the body has been heavily brushed at some time or other by evil, tainted by sorcery or one of the other black arts, participated in or perpetrated exceptional pain. None of these features is necessarily a permanent stain on his soul, and certain writers have sought to clean him up or otherwise to redeem him. The brand of the beast must be evident at least as background coloration for Hitler to be our Hitler, though; otherwise, all our efforts to mine him for metaphor would fail.

Mostly they fail anyway and will go on failing, one obvious reason being the easy reversion to formulaic writing too many writers have taken. The procedure was described a few years ago by Bruce McCall in an *Esquire* article entitled "The Hitler Formula: Out of the Ashes of WWII and onto the Best Seller List in 14 Easy Steps." The steps are the expected ones and mandate inclusion of various Nazi props (dagger, armband, eagle, pistol, whip), personalities (Hitler, Himmler, Goebbels, Göring, Bormann, et al.), settings (office, bunker, ghetto, U-boat, death camp), crimes (by pistol, phenol, hanging, guard dog, gas). There is little that is not predictable in this kind of fiction just as there is little in it that is worth pondering or paying for. Yet presumably somebody buys it, reads it, and goes back for more of the same. Otherwise, we would not have it in the first place, and much shelf space in our airports, drug stores, and other public places would be denuded of its omnipresent array of swastikas, jackboots, leather capes, and other popular iconography of World War II.

It is clear from these publications that Hitler is evolving into a fiction, an evolution that found sensational expression in the spring of 1983. In retrospect, it should have come as no surprise that this year, which marked the fiftieth anniversary of Hitler's rise to political power, should have produced something extra special, but no one was prepared for the truly "big" news that was in the works and was soon to rivet the attention of millions of readers across the continents. I refer, of course, to "Hitler's Diaries."

The degree of money, marketing effort, and general media hype that went into this latest, biggest, and boldest attempt to sell Hitler was unprecedented. Millions of dollars and major international newspapers and magazines were involved, as were scholars with heretofore formidable and fairly unimpeachable credentials. Preceded by an advertising campaign of lavish proportions and accompanied by a series of "news breaks" calculated to awaken interest by establishing a climate of monumental expectation, the first installments of "Hitler's Diaries" were published almost simultaneously in Germany, England, and the United States and drew a generous amount of journalistic attention elsewhere around the world.

To be sure, the attention was mixed, and more than a little skepticism accompanied the first news about the diaries' discovery and their imminent publication. Nothing sells like controversy, though, and it quickly became clear that the market could make good use of any early doubts that were to be raised about the authenticity of the new Hitler material. "Hitler's Diaries: Are They Genuine?" *Newsweek* asked on the cover of its May 2, 1983 number, but before an answer could be given the magazine's promotions office had already settled the issue through copy it ran in expensive full-page advertisements in the *New York Times* and the *Washington Post*. Here is some of what *Newsweek* had to say in these ads:

> In 1945 the world thought it had heard the last of Adolf Hitler.
> But this week *Newsweek* presents a special report on Hitler's Secret Diaries.
> In 1945 the personal diaries of Adolf Hitler—over 57 handwritten volumes—were carried out of the Fuehrer-bunker during the final days of the Third Reich.
> Mysteriously, these diaries passed from one hiding place to another. From a steel trunk which survived a plane crash during a last minute escape from Berlin, to somewhere in East Germany, to a vault in a Swiss Bank.
> And the world never knew of their existence.
> Just as mysteriously, the diaries recently surfaced. . . .
> These controversial papers could rewrite the history of the Third

Reich from Hitler's rise to power to his suicide in the ruins of Berlin. They shed new light on his character, his plans for war, Munich, the miracle of Dunkirk, the flight of Rudolf Hess, his military campaigns, his relations to his lover, Eva Braun. And they raise some disturbing questions about his role in the Final Solution.

Even as this copy was being written, senior editors at *Newsweek* suspected the "Hitler Diaries" were a sensational fraud, but they went ahead anyway with their May 2 special number, whose cover featured the standard photograph of Hitler at the height of his power, right arm outstretched in rigid salute, left arm emblazoned with a large, bright swastika, chest covered heroically with an Iron Cross. Whatever the text inside would say, these symbols on the cover had already spoken their message: Nazi iconography remained compellingly alive and by itself would direct attention all over again to the mad years of Hitler's rule. The captions accompanying the Führer's proud pose nudged the reader's imagination along a little more: "How [the Diaries] Could Rewrite History," one teased, and another, more simply but more enticingly still, "Hitler and the Jews." As for the issue of whether or not the texts of the purported diaries were genuine and deserved to be brought before the reading public in such a manner, a single line in the *Newsweek* story laid that matter to rest: "Now the appearance of Hitler's diaries—genuine or not, it almost doesn't matter in the end—reminds us of the horrible reality on which our doubts about ourselves, and each other, are based." Whatever the second half of this sentence might mean, the first half made it clear that, fact or fiction, the diaries somehow had an ultimate claim on our attention and that *Newsweek* was doing the reading public a service by reporting on them at such length and thereby reopening the historic debate about Nazism.

Because of the intercontinental nature of the enterprise, the debate was taking place simultaneously in Germany and England, thanks to even more generous publication of "Hitler's Diaries" by *Stern,* the West German illustrated weekly news magazine that originally acquired them, and by the *Sunday Times* of London. News weeklies in France *(Paris Match)* and Italy *(Panorama)* were also planning to run excerpts from the diaries. The *Star,* like the London *Sunday Times* another paper in the Murdoch chain, would carry the diaries to a popular readership in the United States, as would similar tabloids elsewhere.

Questions about history require historians, of course, and some very notable ones were bound to let their voices be heard, among them, not surprisingly, Hugh Trevor-Roper. What astonished in his case, though, was not that he entered the debate but that he entered it so quickly on the side of the London *Sunday Times* and, putting aside the historian's customary caution, peremptorily pronounced the diaries to be genuine. Since Trevor-Roper has long been recognized as a scholar who speaks with authority about Hitler, his instant endorsement of the diaries' authenticity ("I'm staking my reputation on it") seemed to put the skeptics momentarily on the defensive and to award the publications a legitimacy they otherwise would not have won so readily. Trevor-Roper was joined in his endorsement by David Irving, a right-wing historian of the Nazi period who put aside some initial doubts and, after first deriding the whole affair, later also publicly stated his belief that the diaries were in fact written by Hitler.

One or two others let down their scholarly guard and likewise seemed to lend a measure of credence to the claims trumpeted by *Stern* and others that the literary goods they had were genuine. Shortly thereafter, though, when other historians and handwriting experts entered the fray, and when it became known that Trevor-Roper had seen only a small sample of the texts, and that for only a few hours, doubts were voiced more confidently and apologies began to be prepared. Within a matter of days Trevor-Roper, who, it became known, served the *Sunday Times* as one of its directors, retracted his hasty words of endorsement and formally admitted his mistake ("I'm extremely sorry"). And within a few more days specialists at West Germany's Federal Archives at Koblenz and at the offices of the Federal Criminal Police in Wiesbaden conclusively exposed the "Hitler Diaries" for the fraud that many people suspected them to be from the start.

Whatever else one might conclude about this latest episode in the fictionalization of Adolf Hitler, it is clear that a large audience remains fascinated by Hitler and that any new revelations about him, however apocryphal, will have little trouble finding receptive readers. The British historian Geoffrey Barraclough tried to dampen some of that enthusiasm a short time back in a piece he wrote entitled "Goodbye, Hitler," in which he set forth the view that enough has already been said, and it is time now to turn attention elsewhere. This attitude is understandable, in some ways even admirable, but it does not acknowledge the obvious hold that Hitler continues to have over very large numbers of people in Europe and the United States, who remain hungry for still another tale about Hitler, especially if it involves his odd affair with Eva Braun or his murderous affair with the Jews. For this reason, Barraclough's commendable rationalism will not do.

In fact, it does not seem as if historical explanation, at whatever length and of whatever degree of sophistication, will soon succeed in putting the man to rest. His ghost remains elusive and haunts the minds and imaginations of millions, a fact that the young Trevor-Roper grasped almost forty years ago when he lamented that "reason is powerless against the obstinate love of fiction" and that no amount of historical evidence will prevent "the rise of a myth, if a myth is wanted." Add to the love of fiction the love of money or the desire to engage in some particularly nasty political manipulation and the growth of the Hitler myth is not so difficult to understand. If anything, the likelihood is that it will be with us still for many years to come, at times as a self-evident fiction, at other times more covertly disguised as a revelation of new fact.

Because we necessarily look to professional historians to help us sort out the differences between fact and fiction, one of the most distressing aspects of the "Hitler Diaries" fraud was the role played by Trevor-Roper. To be sure, he hastily offered public statements of apology, but he of all people should never have been party to counterfeit publications about Hitler in the first place, especially by a news corporation to which he had a professional connection. David Irving, the author of a revisionist history of the Nazi period, *Hitler's War*, which argues that Hitler was not primarily responsible for the Holocaust of the Jews and which almost all German historians regard as something of an elaborate fiction itself, did not have much of a reputation to lose and came out of the affair with the same standing he had before it began—a highly dubious one. The handwriting experts, paper analysts, and bookbinder inspectors walked away with all of the orchids. In the end, therefore, the disciplines of mind demanded by the exercise of responsible history prevailed over the desires and fabrications of the fictive imagination.

But not for very long, for almost concurrently with the publication and subsequent exposé of the "Hitler Diaries," William Morrow and Company brought out a new novel by Richard Hugo entitled *The Hitler*

Diaries. The confusion that normally besets the student of the Nazi period seemed as nothing compared to what confronted him as a result of the simultaneous appearance of "Hitler's Diaries" and *The Hitler Diaries,* the first passed off as a series of "historical documents" now known to have been a gigantic fraud, the second a fiction about the possible historicity of very similar documents suspected of being fraudulent. Unless one was willing to put so much happenstance on the imponderable ways of the *Zeitgeist,* it almost seemed necessary to wonder who was doing what to whom. And why?

As novels of international intrigue go, Hugo's book made for entertaining reading, but coming as it did on the heels of the *Stern* affair, most readers probably wondered just what kind of book they were holding in their hands. There was no mistaking it as a novel, but it was a novel that too closely resembled the news in yesterday's *Sunday Times* and the recent special numbers of *Newsweek.* The book's protagonist, for instance, is an English historian of Nazi Germany in the employ of a publishing firm, who is charged with verifying the authenticity of manuscripts purported to be nothing less than Hitler's secret diaries. Trevor-Roper is named by name in the novel, and a bit of him peeks through the central character, who otherwise resembles a cross between David Irving and Sam Spade. This historian *cum* literary detective is promised a sizable sum of money if he delivers positive verification of the diaries' authenticity, a good deal less if he withholds his scholarly imprimatur and pronounces the manuscript a fraud. Yet whether the manuscripts prove to be fact or fiction, the New York publisher who is offered them by an elegantly mysterious German agent already knows that he has been given "the hottest thing in publishing since the war." "Thinking about big money, about films," the publisher adds up how much he might expect to gain from selling serial rights to newspapers and magazines around the world, and, in a version of *Newsweek's* "genuine or not, it almost doesn't matter in the end," decides to go ahead with the deal. Here is a representative excerpt from the text, one that features a dialogue between the publisher, Magruder, and his partner, Hirsch:

> 'With that sort of fantasy pornokitsch it's got to be a fake. It's too good to be true. . . .'
> 'I guess so,' Magruder said, 'Anyway, for now it doesn't matter. . . .'

'You could try finding out whether it's authentic.'

'I think I know the answer to that one. It may be more interesting to discover just how good a fake it is. But then what? . . . It still beats every book on record I ever heard of. . . .'

'Let's say we can persuade people the diaries are genuine: then what do we have?' He thought for a moment and then said, 'You know, if I had to think of a book that everybody in the world would want to read, then this would be it.'

In sum, genuine or not, "We'd have the book of the century on our hands," as one of Magruder's colleagues puts it. *The Hitler Diaries* was surely not going to be the book of the century, but together with *Stern*'s and *Newsweek*'s "Hitler Diaries" it drove home the obvious appeal of writing of all sorts—credible, incredible, it-almost-doesn't-matter-in-the-end—about the Third Reich. As Magruder says about his Hitler diary, hoax or not, "anyone who believes in the Bermuda Triangle will buy it. . . . I don't see how we can miss."

As the publishers gain, much of the reading public—gullible, eager to feed irrational appetites, ready and willing to be taken in—loses and has been losing for some time now. The marketing of Adolf Hitler has become big business, and in no small part it has become a commercially compromised and politically mischievous business. To what degree minds are being changed as dollars are being won no one can know for certain, but the fictionalization of history carries with it a certain price to be paid through the generations. With respect to Hitler the price is an especially heavy one, for as he gains his release from historical memory and enters the open spaces of fictive imaginings, he will take on the shapes of various competing mythologies, some of which have a major stake in absolving him of his worst crimes. As an indication of what happens to the historical sense as the processes of mythification take over, one can hardly do better than to note the following episode from Daniel Lang's *A Backward Look: Germans Remember:*

> Haupts [Leo Haupts, a professor of modern history at Cologne University] had known of the deportation of Jews during the war, he told me, but that was all. He said he had known nothing about concentration camps. He didn't envy Germans who had, he said—they probably lived with a guilty conscience. I asked Michael [his son] whether any legacy of guilt had come down to young Germans, and he shook his head. "Why

should it?" he demanded indignantly. "We weren't even born!" His spirited reply drew a nod of approval from his father, and the two exchanged a smile, their abjuration of guilt a bond between them. Mrs. Haupts watched them, relieved. His detachment back, Haupts said good-naturedly that he wondered whether concentration camps were destined to be remembered. In time, the professor observed, facts could turn fuzzy, lending themselves to revision. He cited an example. Among historians, he informed me, it had long been accepted that Charlemagne had decapitated four thousand Saxons in the eighth century for stealing cattle from the Franks. Well, Haupts said, in recent years some historians had been leaning toward the view that the Saxons had not been massacred but merely banished. Haupts concluded, "It's only speculation, of course, but it may be that there will come a day when people will ask, 'Were there really concentration camps, or was that just a myth?'"

Professor Haupts recalls to mind a character in Richard Hugo's novel who argues that "history is a court whose judgments are always appealed. . . . Napoleon was condemned and reviled, but history had come to recognize that he was a great man." With enough sensationalizing publications about Hitler, the ranks of the great may soon increase, and one can imagine a day not too far off when at least some people will ask, "Was he really so monstrous a fellow?"

II

From Facts to Fictions

The dead can be more dangerous
than the living.
—H. R. TREVOR-ROPER

AS IS EVIDENT from all that has been said thus far, Hitler is evolving into a fiction, a fiction that sometimes bears little resemblance to historical fact. This is not to say that writers drawn to him are altogether uninterested in his life and career but that in appropriating episodes from the life they are mostly interested in making an appeal to one or another of the regnant fantasies about Nazism. In their rawest form these fantasies tend to reduce to exaggerated dreams of power and submission, with greater or lesser emphasis on the pleasures and pains of erotic conquest and the pornography of violence, all usually imagined against the backdrop of a quasi-religious political messianism and a reawakened antisemitism. One can expect the blood to run pretty freely in fictions that stimulate such rough dreams as these, and in the common run of pulp literature, in which the face of menace is palpable, that is what one finds. In the more literary books these same fantasies are released in subtler, more controlled fashion, but they are often present all the same. Whatever the degree of overt or covert representation, though, in virtually every case it is the mythological Hitler, and not primarily the historical one, that seems most alive and continues to feed the reading public's appetite for images of the Third Reich.

According to one recent report, "the trade in Nazi memorabilia—genuine and fake—currently grosses upwards of $50 million a year worldwide and involves more than 50,000 collectors, most of them Americans." It is also in America where many of the publications about Nazism—scholarly, commercial, and apologetic—are to be found, where most of the films and television programs are produced, where the popular literature industry seems to be able to sell almost any book with a swastika on its cover, where much of the new wave of antisemitica originates.

To be sure, one can find similar manifestations in the European countries and in parts of South America and the Middle East, but Americans seem to show an unflagging interest in the Nazi era, and American popular culture remains highly receptive to stories and images of the Third Reich. Why is this so? Apart from the fact that large numbers of Americans fought against Nazi Germany, what is it about the Hitler era, and not, say, the Stalin era or the reign of terror under Mao, that is so compelling? In terms of sheer political villainy, at least as measured by the numbers killed, the Soviet and the Chinese tyrannies surpassed that of Hitler, yet there is little resonant myth that attaches to the names of Stalin and Mao in this country, and images of them are hardly to be found on our T.V. screens or in our popular fiction. What is it about Hitler—and Hitler alone—that makes him stand out among twentieth-century tyrants and awards him primacy of place in the contemporary imagination of political brutality?

The first place not to look for an answer to these questions is in the conventional formula about man's inhumanity to man, which is invoked whenever the crimes of the Third Reich are mentioned. The moral reflex is understandable but the rhetoric too banal to mean much anymore. One can, after all, find ample illustration of the inhumane in any day's *New York Times* or Chicago *Tribune* and need not appeal to the grossities of Nazism as testament to brutal behavior, for such behavior has by now become part of the familiar round of daily life. Even if that were not the case, though, the slaughters carried out by the regimes of Stalin and Mao offer as much evidence of mass cruelty as does the Hitler regime, and yet the Russian and Chinese murderers have not seized the moral imagination in nearly so tenacious a way as the Nazi murderer has. For all of its intended seriousness, then, there is good reason to suspect that the moral truism about man's inhumanity to man is not sufficient to explain the hold that Hitler continues to have over us.

Neither is that second familiar touchstone sufficient, namely the often-quoted dictum of Santayana that he who forgets the past is doomed to repeat it. The aphorism sounds right, and one would not want to quarrel with its basic wisdom, but its application is much too selective to explain why the history of Hitler's crimes is remembered while that of other recent tyrannies goes largely ignored. The chastening effect of historical memory alone, therefore, would not seem to be enough to account for the dominant place that Hitler has assumed in contemporary consciousness.

Where, then, is one to look for answers? Geography and cultural mythology provide at least partial sources of explanation, and in some oblique way one might even look to theology. The geographical factor is obvious enough: as "Orientals," Stalin and Mao are both exotic to the Western imagination, and their crimes, no matter how extreme, fit some general notion that the West has long held about the inherent barbarism of the East. Attila the Hun and Genghis Khan stand behind them as archetypes and purportedly can explain their savagery, which anyway took place far from Western shores and did not consume populations that intimately touch the nerve of fellow feeling. In these respects not even the noble sentiments roused by "man's inhumanity to man" come very prominently into play, for the humanity destroyed in such large numbers did not closely enough resemble the familiar run of man, woman, and child to evoke very much of either pity or fear. The decimation of Asiatics by other Asiatics, in other words, is not conceived of as part of a closely shared history and is neither passionately argued over nor very specifically retained. Gruesome it may have been, but it is generally regarded, if at all, as somebody else's affair.

Not so the slaughter brought on by Hitler, which happened in countries populated by kindred people, implicated our own direct bloodlines, and brought to a point of still unresolved crisis the basic values of our common civilization. These formulas offend by their anthropological crudeness and simplicity, it is true, but they also help to explain a crucial difference in judgments about the Nazi program of genocide and the Stalinist and Maoist mass killings. Theoretically, sympathy should flow evenly over all the world's corpses, but in fact it does not, and to this day the tens of millions of Russian and Chinese victims go largely unremembered and unmourned in the West. Their deaths, largely anonymous and engineered for reasons that are vaguely taken to be internal to the national politics of distant and alien lands, awaken no metaphysical questions, have no significant resonance in legal, theological, or imaginative literature, evoke no ongoing discussions about the moral deformities of the age or the death of God. That is not the way it should be, admittedly, only the way it is.

When one turns, though, to the horrors brought on by Hitler, all of the categories of feeling, judgment, imagination, and value change dramatically. So, too, does our sense of personality and the power it wields. Unlike the silent, hidden, and generally imponderable personalities that masked the sinister sides of Stalin and Mao, Hitler was flamboyant, theatrical, overstated, omnipresent. Moreover, our perception of him, in contrast to our perception of the others, is that he had the German masses behind him—those cheering, waving, adoring millions pictured in the newsreels as being always at the pitch of enthusiasm before their Führer. Hitler not only terrorized, he led, and his party's public rallies attracted very large numbers of eager and exuberant followers. Thus, Nazism is seen as a mass movement of loyal and passionately dedicated supporters, a whole nation on the march behind their Führer. What shocks, of course, is the familiar faces in the crowd, the look of neighborly, even family, resemblance. Everybody looks so clean, so shiny, so much the happy embodiment of the popular Nordic ideal. The thought that somehow *these* people were complicit with Hitler in his crimes stuns the moral centers of imagination in a way that does not happen when one recalls the Gulag or other atrocities of the twentieth century, atrocities that may have been fully as hideous in their nature and extent but that do not seem to have carried the endorsement of the popular will. Nazi Germany was different, though, for throughout most of his reign Hitler had a sizable portion of the citizenry behind him.

How did he manage to whip them up and win them over, get them marching and singing, send them off in the millions to kill and be killed? One can, to be sure, raise similar questions about any nationalist movement, but one does not, at least not in the first instance. For displays of patriotic passion, discipline, loyalty, fervor, and sheer public spectacle, primacy of place belongs to German National Socialism. Yet precisely how did Hitler manage to work his will over so large and so civilized a nation as Germany, a nation that in so many ways stood at the center of Western cultural self-definition? What madness or magic did he use? Unless one is engaged professionally in the study of comparative politics, one does not ask these questions about anyone but Hitler, at least not until one has first asked them about him. In this respect, as in so many others, it is he who defines the essence, the dynamics, and, thus far, the extravagant limits of modern political extremity.

To use the word "political" here is to situate Hitler naturally enough within the history of his time but not very precisely within the imagination of that time as it has found expression in so much of postwar literature. For politics implies not only the organization and implementation of power but also its rational control and the systematic ordering of credible and achievable priorities. After a certain point in his career, though, it becomes impossible to understand some of the deepest intentions of Hitler's political program or even to see them as "political" in the conventional sense of that term, and it is not primarily as a leader rationally wielding the powers of statecraft that he is remembered today. Rather, Hitler stands before us—feared, detested, yet powerfully recalled—for deeds that transcend the normal political categories and defy political explanation.

At ultimate cost to his nation, Hitler became the assassin of European Jewry, a role that he pursued with greater passion and consistency than any other and the one above all for which he is remembered today. The matter does not reduce solely to the magnitude of the killings, for, to repeat, Stalin and Mao murdered more; rather, as one ponders the intentions behind the Nazi program of genocide and the means used to carry that program out, one is either perplexed altogether or moved to think in categories that are more metaphysical than political. The contrast with Soviet Russia and China is again instructive. The Stalinist and Maoist mass killings were immense in their proportions, but they nevertheless lend themselves to historical analysis and seem largely explicable in political terms. Thus the enslavement, torture, and murder of millions of Russians and Chinese might be rationalized as part of the internal controls deemed necessary by the Soviet and Chinese dictatorships to eliminate threats posed by the opposition and to keep the masses docile and subservient. The terror, in other words, seems to have been primarily functional, although one would not want to discount psychopathological motives in either case.

Hitler's *Endlösung*, on the other hand, was transnational in scope, served no ostensible strategic or political good, was carried out at the expense of other national programs, and in the end contributed to the disgrace and destruction of the Third Reich. How, then, is one to understand it? Apart from some bogus anthropological theories about racial purity, what is it that drove the Nazis and their allies to institute across an entire continent so ruthless and determined a program of genocide against the Jews?

In the historical literature on Nazism there are innumerable attempts at explanation but no commonly agreed upon answers to these questions. In the realm of imaginative literature, though, this lack of scholarly consensus hardly matters, for what looms largest is the mystery and the madness of the deed itself. In killing the Jews Hitler did something that touched the deep nerve of Western culture, even some secret nerve of sympathy. The killings, and the extensive and highly visible program of anti-Jewish defamation and degradation that preceded them, were revolting, to be sure, but they could find more than a small measure of precedent and even ideological justification in Christian doctrine, long-standing social and political habits of thought, familiar economic and racial arguments, and an ingrained, almost folkloristic bias. Feelings about Jews in European countries were at best always ambivalent, and a history of anti-Jewish persecution preceded Hitler by centuries. In these respects, therefore, if not in others, the Nazi *Endlösung* was just that—not an altogether new departure, but a "final" or ultimate solution to a "problem" that had long irritated the peoples of Europe. Hitler's "solution" was far more radical than any that had heretofore been enacted, but the fact that the Nazis were able to draw upon the active participation of so many, and to render so many more silent and passive witnesses, drives home the point that the massive anti-Jewish terror coincided with and exploited deep-seated popular animosity toward Jews.

In the aftermath of the destructions, though, one still faces a crime that seems largely gratuitous—the fulfillment of some heretofore unsatisfied ideal of killing for the absolute love of killing. Not so much for its numbers, therefore, although they were enormous, or for its political motives, which seem negligible, but for its nihilistic passions and the mythic and almost metaphysical nature of its design does the Nazi *Endlösung* stand out from other crimes of the century.

At its center stands Hitler, who can be explained no more completely or convincingly in political terms than he can be in psychological, sociological, or philosophical terms. One can call him a tyrant and a megalomaniac, a psychopath and a monster, a devil and an anti-Christ, but each of these figures is much too weak to contain him, and in the end he stands before us as a singularly fearsome figure of limitless destructive will. Those around him—Himmler, Göring, Goebbels, Hess, Heydrich, Eichmann, Kaltenbrunner, Mengele, Speer—are somewhat more accessible to reasoned explanation, although there are aspects of each that are also elusive. For present purposes, though, which is to say for purposes of understanding their appropriation by imaginative writers, what is important is that they continue to exist at all as living figures of the Nazi era. Eichmann, for instance, is a central figure in several plays, Göring shows up at his most bizarre in numerous pulp novels, Mengele's name is invoked almost as often as Auschwitz itself is, and Speer has evolved into a figure of prominent and almost respectable intellectual standing. By contrast, who can name the colleagues-in-arms of Mao or conjure images of Stalin's chief aides? One knows only vaguely that they existed, carried out orders, and performed the murderous work of their regimes, but outside of scholarly studies they have no afterlife in literature and do not occupy prominent places in popular imagination.

Hitler and his henchmen, on the other hand, continue to appear and reappear on the large and small screens of our homes and movie houses and fill the pages of popular literature. Far from fading back into the past, they have emerged as a primary code of our cultural mythology, a code that has its own distinctive vocabulary, recognizable symbol system, ordered hierarchy, significant place names, familiar songs and slogans, established manner of dress. We are, in other words, in possession of, and in no small manner possessed by, a whole world of resonant meaning, replete with its own sources of pathos and signification and evocative of a life that has far from run its course. If anything, the imaginative landscape of Nazism continues to expand and increasingly has come to shape the way we see the world, defining not only the ruins of our recent past but, one fears, part of the gruesome and almost unthinkable prospect ahead.

This is not the way things were to have turned out. One of the hopes of the earliest historians of Nazi Germany was to dispel the legends that had surrounded Hitler and to expose his Reich for what it was, thus preventing, so far as it was possible to prevent, the rebirth of a Hitler myth.

Ironically enough, though, and often as a result of the efforts of historians and others, a new mythopoeia began to develop almost as soon as pen touched paper. The work of Hugh Trevor-Roper is a case in point.

As an officer in British intelligence, Trevor-Roper was assigned the task of investigating and writing up the last weeks of Hitler's life. To do that, he was given access to a wealth of documentary material as well as to captured German prisoners of war in the Allied zones, and from these sources he was able to learn most of what he needed to know about events in the Führerbunker during the final days of the war. His aim, as he wrote, was "to prevent (as far as such means can prevent) the rebirth of the Hitler myth," by which he meant chiefly to discourage any belief that Hitler might somehow have survived the war and would soon be stirring again. The Russians had begun to put out ambiguous reports about conditions at the bunker, which did not conclusively confirm or deny Hitler's suicide. Thus the challenge to Allied intelligence, a challenge that the young Trevor-Roper took up and more than adequately met in his reconstruction of "the true history of [Hitler's] life and his melodramatic and carefully stage-managed end."

The book was a success from the day of its publication and was hailed by most reviewers as the final word on its subject. Moreover, in addition to praise for its fine use of the historical evidence at hand, it was widely admired for its literary qualities, as a work "which has all the excitement of dramatic intrigue, but doubled and tripled, . . . a book which shames fiction by proving how infinitely more strange and incredible facts can be." In reading it, as one contemporary reviewer wrote, "our imagination rises to a great and terrible story," the story of "an inhuman madman" who "must be numbered among the most dynamic men of all recorded history." This response to Trevor-Roper's work was typical of that of most reviewers and points to an inherent contradiction between the scholar's aims and his readers' reactions right from the start: in writing so vividly and so well about Hitler's end, Trevor-Roper would "set the seal on Nuremberg" and, at the same time, whether he intended it or not, stimulate new levels of imaginative interest in this man who was spoken of as having "had the power of a god or a devil." His book, in other words, would, by its very nature, both dampen and excite a new Hitler myth.

In part, it is in the nature of narrative as narrative to evoke such mixed responses, for writing is an establishing act and, when well done, awards all the possibilities of a second life to the subject it sets out to reconstitute. In the case of Hitler, the temptations of mythopoeia were especially strong, for life had been consciously molded by art, or at least by the gestures of art, since the beginning of his career in the 1920s, so that it was never easy to see the man through the metaphorical screen that had been so elaborately erected to present him as an extraordinary figure. For years he had been hailed as "leader" and "lord," as "another Luther," and even as a "Messiah . . . sent to us by God in order to save Germany." Not all of the epithets were affirmative, to be sure, for he was also called "tyrant" and "dictator," "madman" and "megalomaniac." The point is, whether seen as savior or scourge, Hitler was constantly imagined in tropes that awarded him a larger-than-life presence, an image that he and his leading propagandists carefully cultivated and that even his enemies contributed to by the figures of speech they used to describe him.

Trevor-Roper, for all of his intentions to establish the "facts" of Hitler's final period, was no less given to figurative conceptions of his subject than others who had tried to envision the Führer. Thus *The Last Days of Hitler* is filled with phrases that refer to "that demonic genius" and "dreadful master," "the Angel of Destruction" and "God of Destruction." In Trevor-Roper's view, Hitler was not primarily a politician but "by nature an artist," and the art he practiced and brought to a terrible perfection was that of human destruction. Consequently, he was described as a "Moloch" and "Pharaoh," an insatiable and evil "deity" lusting after "human sacrifices." This kind of religious language pervades the narrative and more than anything else establishes Hitler's career within the codes of a stridently militant and basically malevolent theology. Nazism is defined as "the religion of the German revolution" and Hitler not only as a "revolutionary genius" but as the revolution's mad "Messiah," "a cannibal god" with a "terrible appetite for blood." In keeping with these figures, his aides are referred to as "priests" and "prophets," who would be prone to "bow in unfeigned adoration before the god into whose presence [they] had been admitted." The "god" is pictured as being full of rages, a figure of thundering anger whose will was not to be crossed, although on occasion he could also show himself to be gentle and forgiving. For the most part, though, he is imagined within this set of rhetorical configurations as a driven and pitiless destroyer, the unchallenged lord of a revolutionary nihilism.

When Trevor-Roper wishes to vary these images, he does so either by reconstituting Hitler as an oriental and not an occidental leader or by placing him within the occult terms of parapsychology. Thus Hitler's administrative circle is described as an "exotic" or "oriental court," his aides as "the satraps of the court," their activities as part of a new "Byzantine palace-politics," the whole tenor of political activity in Berlin as more characteristic of some "oriental sultanate" than of a modern Western government. The will to deny Hitler Western origins is exceptionally strong in Trevor-Roper's book and is expressed in some of the author's most powerfully rendered passages:

> It was always understood that Hitler would remain true to his original programme, *Weltmacht oder Niedergang*—world-power or ruin. If world-power was unattainable, then . . . he would make the ruin as great as he could, and himself, like Samson at Gaza, perish in the cataclysm of his own making. For Hitler was not a figure of Western Europe, however he sought to pose as its champion against Asiatic Bolshevism; nor did his melodramatic character respond to the Confucian ideal of a tidy, unobtrusive death. When he envisaged himself against an historical background, when his imagination was heated, and his vanity intoxicated, with flattery and success, and he rose from his modest supper of vegetable pie and distilled water to prance upon the table and identify himself with the great conquerors of the past, it was not as Alexander, or Caesar, or Napoleon that he wished to be celebrated, but as the re-embodiment of those angels of destruction—of Alaric, the sacker of Rome, of Attila, "the scourge of God," of Genghis Khan, the leader of the Golden Horde.

This is inspired, almost celebratory prose, and quite clearly makes of the "history" of Hitler's final days a fiction of folkloric dimensions. Although Trevor-Roper might have set out to establish the "facts" in the case, it is evident from passages like this one that he, too, could not altogether resist the symbolic lure of his subject, and he was to contribute his share to some of the more striking aspects of the Hitler legend.

The legend was to be shaped as well by a fascination with the most irrational sides of Hitler's personality, and to describe these Trevor-Roper took recourse not only to the language of biblical theology and Middle Eastern and oriental legend but to the special language of the occult sciences. Thus Hitler is described repeatedly as a "wizard" and "enchanter," a leader who could command unconditional obedience from his subjects because of "the mesmeric influence" he had over them. It is odd to observe a historian using language of this sort, especially a historian whose avowed purpose was to establish his subject on the basis of verifiable evidence and thus "to prevent the rebirth of a myth." In writing about the more compelling sides of Hitler's character, however, the fiction writer within the scholar seemed to come alive and to find release in prose that once more is memorable for its descriptive color:

> The fascination of those eyes, which had bewitched so many seemingly sober men—which had exhausted Speer, and baffled Rauschning, and seduced Stumpfegger, and convinced an industrialist that he had direct telepathic communication with the Almighty—had not deserted them. . . . Hitler had the eyes of a hypnotist which seduced the wits and affections of all who yielded to their power. . . . This personal magnetism remained with him to the end; and only by reference to it can we explain the extraordinary obedience which he still commanded in the last week of his life, when all the machinery of force and persuasion had disappeared . . . and only his personality remained.

However else one might choose to account for Hitler's power, in this author's understanding of it the elements of sorcery were too prominent to be denied. "The power of the Fuehrer was a magic power," Trevor-Roper writes at one point, "and no profane hand might reach out to touch it until the reigning priest was really dead." It was a power that exercised itself as a "hypnotic influence" and "compelling enchantment," "a spell wherewith the whole German people had been bewitched." Trevor-Roper took over much of this kind of talk from Speer, under whose influence he, like so many others after him, seems to have partially and temporarily fallen. The result for the "true history" that he was writing is obvious enough: some sixth sense, which fiction writers know as inspiration or invention, tended to assert itself strongly and to overcome the sterner and more disciplined historian's sense for factual evidence whenever the question of Hitler's personality arose. At such moments Hitler appeared as the "German Messiah," Goebbels and Bormann as his "high-priests," Himmler as his "Grand Inquisitor." Or, to capture the Führer's imagined "eastern" flavor, he was "the new Pharaoh" or "a new, more permanent Genghis Khan." Finally, to return to the language of the occult, he might be glimpsed as the compelling centerpoint of some "magic circle" that he created with "the mysterious intensity of those dull,

glaucous eyes" and "the messianic egotism of that harsh, oracular voice."
Whichever way, Hitler emerges in Trevor-Roper's book in strongly
mythological terms as "the modern destroyer of mankind" who "wished to
be sent with human sacrifices to his grave."

This is not to suggest that there is no sober description or analytic
interpretation in *The Last Days of Hitler,* for there is plenty of both, but
rather that historical exposition vies with and frequently is overcome by
figuration of the kind that one finds more typically in fictive accounts of
mythic heroes or legendary stories of saints and devils. In the end, therefore, one retains from a reading of this book images both of the worn-
down, miserable suicide and of the "cannibal god, rejoicing in the ruin of
his own temples"—the "real-life" Hitler, documented as faithfully as the
working historian could transcribe him, and the imagined Hitler,
transmuted in mythical shapes that would live on beyond the grave.

In the epilogue to *The Last Days of Hitler* Trevor-Roper could state,
with some reasonable degree of confidence, that whereas in the future
"Nazism may revive" and "a new party may appeal to a myth of Hitler," it
would have to be "to a myth of Hitler dead, not of Hitler living." In the
preface to the 1962 edition of his book, looking back at what he had
accomplished some fifteen years earlier, he again could take satisfaction in
his conclusions: "Nothing has happened to cause me to alter a word I have
written. . . . Hitler remains dead . . . and no one now doubts his death."
In the literal sense, the historian's summation is true, but in the figurative
sense—which is to say, in the sense that historical personages may take on
a posthumous life in literature—precisely the opposite is true. Despite
the historian's labors, and at times even because of them, versions of
Hitler have survived the man's death in the bunker of Berlin and today
comprise a myth that seems to become more and not less omnipresent
with the passage of time.

While it would be incorrect to suggest that *The Last Days of Hitler* has
been the prime source for the evolution of this myth, it has fed into it in
ways that its young author could not have anticipated. In the forty years
since Trevor-Roper first published the results of his historical investiga-
tions, his work has been the point of departure for virtually all later
imaginings of Hitler's end. Among writers who have sought to rewrite the
more controversial aspects of the final days of Hitler's life, Trevor-Roper's
book has been the major statement to contend with. It is referred to by

name in more than one fiction and quoted in prefatory inscriptions to novels. What is more, and of special interest to this study, the author has himself been fictionalized in some of the more recent Hitler books, appearing at times under his own name, more often as the thinly veiled prototype of the successful historian-sleuth in search of fugitive leaders of the Third Reich. Both Trevor-Roper and his book, in other words, are beginning to take on fictive shapes and have already become recognizable ciphers within the evolving corpus of imaginative literature about Hitler.

It is ironic, and to the professional historian no doubt an affront, that this development should have occurred, but anyone who appreciates the way the literary imagination works will not have much difficulty explaining it. *The Last Days of Hitler* has taken hold precisely because Trevor-Roper was the first to imagine himself so exhaustively into the most intimate circumstances of Hitler's final and most ruinous period. He did so with the historian's openness to the available facts but also with the writer's desire to vivify those facts and to weave them into a story that would transcend the fragmentary and random character of documentary sources, a story with its own pace, development, color, and denouement. From the scholar's side, always the side of the skeptic, this story, and especially its self-destructive ending, might be pronounced melodramatic, but from the writer's side it was to take on something of the brilliance of aesthetic shape and to fascinate in ways that surpassed the empirical procedures of an investigative report.

The fact is, Trevor-Roper did far more than clarify the circumstances surrounding Hitler's death: in some deeply imaginative sense, he entered Hitler's death chambers and, with the novelist's eye for physical detail and psychological nuance, reconstructed the madness and the poignancy of the Führer's last moments. He did so not to award any honor to Hitler's suicide or to dignify it as one would a hero's death, but, like any good mystery writer in search of the smoking gun, he revealed an abiding enough fascination with his subject to make it *interesting*—the clearest indication that Hitler would survive his own death.

III

In and Out of History

> Art knows nothing of history, but
> helps itself to its terror.
>
> —René Char

THE NOTION THAT Hitler survived his own death offends, both for the obscene nature of the wish it seems to represent and for its obvious assault on what we take to be historical truth. For reasons of moral as well as psychic well-being, it is best that we maintain belief in the man's suicide and go about our affairs relieved that the world is rid of him. Yet, the question is still sometimes asked, did Hitler indeed die in his Berlin bunker? As far as we know—which is to say, as far as our best historians have been able to tell us on the evidence available to them—he did. There have been disputes among scholars as to whether he shot himself through the mouth or through the temple and also over his use of poison, but no responsible historian today contests Hitler's death by his own hand on April 30, 1945. It is well established that Eva Braun died with him and that both their bodies were burnt in the garden outside the bunker, according to orders given by Hitler earlier. One can take *The Last Days of Hitler*, as well as any of a number of more recent accounts of Hitler's end by other historians of Nazi Germany, therefore, as being as reliable a death certificate as we are ever likely to have in the direct absence of a corpse. However, because we cannot today point to the man's grave and say with certainty, there he lies, one comes to see what Trevor-Roper meant when he wrote years ago, "Hitler achieved his last ambition. Like Alaric, buried secretly under the river-bed of Busento, the modern destroyer of mankind is now immune from discovery."

This statement is true only in the literal sense. In the literary sense—in the sense that semblances of life are revived through imaginative interpretation, invention, and all the other forms of fictive realization—the "discovery" of Adolf Hitler has been an ongoing process for some forty years now. As far back as 1939, the English novelist Wyndham Lewis, himself the author of one of the earliest and most outrageously partisan books about Hitler ever written, could declare:

> Thousands of books about Hitler have poured out of the printing presses of Europe and America. There is no scrap of information about him that has not been made public; there is nothing he has ever said or done, or that his parents or grandparents ever said or did, that has not been reported. As a subject Herr Hitler has been exhausted as no subject has ever been exhausted before.

This in 1939, no less—years before the real Hitler wave even began to ripple. Some eight years earlier, when Lewis published the first of his several embarrassingly bad books on Nazism, he was brimming with praise for the German Führer as a "Man of Peace" and "a sort of inspired and eloquent Everyman." Lewis went on:

> It is essential to understand that Adolf Hitler is not a sabre-rattler at all. . . . I do not think that if Hitler had his way he would bring the fire and the sword across otherwise peaceful frontiers. He would, I am positive, remain peacefully at home, fully occupied with the internal problems of the Dritte Reich. . . . The idea, in short, of Germany being "a military menace" can be entirely dismissed from the most apprehensive mind. . . .

Lewis did not set out to write about Hitler as a fiction, at least not intentionally so, but it is clear from his writings of the 1930s that he was looking at his man through the eyes of a fabulator and making him up as he went along to suit various ideologies then current about the racial purity of "Western White Peoples" and the advantages of class cohesion, noncredit financing, and other anticapitalist, antidemocratic, and antisemitic notions. Lewis was more long-winded and lavish in his praise of Hitler than were most English intellectuals of his day, but he was hardly alone, and one can find similar embarrassments in the political judgments expressed by other prominent writers of the time, including George Bernard Shaw, Ezra Pound, and T. S. Eliot. There were, of course, others who quickly saw Hitler for what he was and tried to explode his image through satire—among them, Brecht in *The Resistable Rise of Arturo Ui,*

A. M. Klein in *The Hitleriad,* and, most memorably, Charlie Chaplin in *The Great Dictator.*

The point is, Wyndham Lewis was preposterously wrong, as he usually was when he wrote about political matters, in pronouncing Hitler "exhausted" as a subject as far back as 1939. If anything, the Third Reich and its leader had barely begun to come into literary focus at the time, this despite the fact that a great deal already had been said by writers of various political and ideological persuasions. Compared to what was to come, though, the contemporary accounts of Hitler and Hitlerism amounted to little more than a clearing of the throat.

A recent satirical piece in *The New Yorker* indicates in a bizarre way the point at which we have arrived today. Ian Frazier's "The Stuttgart Folders" takes off on the opening line of Joseph DiMona's *To the Eagle's Nest* ("Adolf Hitler slipped off his bathrobe and stood naked," called by its author "the most commercial opening line of any novel ever published") and goes on to offer this bit of comic dialogue:

> Himmler swallowed hard. 'You plan to go around like that . . . regularly?' he asked.
> 'Yes, I do. And what of it?'
> 'If I might make so bold as to point out—'
> 'Yes?'
> 'Well, if people saw you, it might . . . it might embarrass the Reich.'
> Hitler looked hard at Himmler for a moment. 'I'm surprised at you, Herr Himmler,' he said quietly. 'I thought you were a man of greater vision. Do we actually care about the Reich?'
> 'No, Führer.'
> 'Do we care whether the Reich lasts a thousand years or twenty minutes?'
> 'No, Führer.'
> 'Do we care in the slightest about this red herring of a war which we have thrown across the path of the non-Aryan world?'
> 'No, Führer.'
> 'What is our real goal, our secret dream that no one else knows? What is this dream that we have dreamed together so many times?'
> 'Our dream is that the Third Reich, in the person of its Führer, Adolf Hitler, shall become the greatest plot device the world has ever known. . . .'

The comic banter may be in bad taste (Himmler and Hitler were simply too viciously cruel to pass as stand-up comedians, even in a *New Yorker* spoof), but otherwise the author gets his point across: as subject matter for fictions of all kinds, Hitler and his Reich draw the imagination more predictably and more powerfully than just about anything else one can think of today. That is an open secret to writers, television producers, and movie makers, who have given the public more versions of Hitler than it can easily absorb.

These fictions might be graphed along two major curves of representation: those that attempt some semblance of historical reconstruction, and those that depart from the historical record to reimagine alternative episodes in the Führer's life and death. Of these two, the latter is by far the more popular with the reading public and therefore the more commonly found, but it will prove helpful to first review some prominent examples of fiction that take an interest in the biographical facts of Hitler's career and give these a new life through narrative extension.

One of the more interesting historical novels about Hitler is Ernst Weiss's little-known book *The Eyewitness*. Written in Paris in 1938 but not published until a quarter of a century later (the German edition first appeared in 1963, an English translation in 1977), the novel portrays a decisive moment in Hitler's early years—the moment of his conversion to political activism. Heavily based on historical materials, *The Eyewitness* employs a narrator modeled on Dr. Edmund Forster, who treated a young Austrian lance corporal for mustard gas poisoning in the year 1918. In the novel, this soldier is never referred to by name but only by initials— A.H.—yet his identity is never in doubt. Like others who fought in the trenches and fell victim to gas warfare, the historical A.H. was temporarily blinded and taken for treatment to a hospital in Pasewalk, in Pomerania. As the novel picks up this story, the narrator-psychiatrist determines that the soldier's pathology is owing more to hysteria than to gas and carries out a cure using deep hypnotic suggestion. The culmination of this treatment, which is portrayed as being heavily spiritual, is A.H.'s dramatic moment of personal and political awakening from a willed blindness.

Will and its workings in political life are at the center of Weiss's interest in the novel, and the author is especially good at depicting the fanatical drive of A.H. on his way to fulfilling his calling as his country's messiah. The best pages in the whole book, in fact, are those devoted to exhibiting the oratorical power of A.H. and the absolute submission of those who listened to him devotedly, obeyed him faithfully, then followed him into a national hysteria more blinding in its effects than the early incapacitation of A. H.:

> He stood above the crowd, for he was untouched by it. . . . He despised it. The crowd, on the other hand, was completely enthralled by him.
>
> He had the habit of speaking only in the evening. Then his listeners were tired, unresisting. They wanted to sleep, dream, be carried away, adore, obey blindly, be possessed by the spirit. Hardly anyone was left untouched, for he intoxicated himself. He showed everyone how glorious it was to be possessed of a single, powerful, worldly idea. . . . He wanted this joy. His emotion worked on our emotion. . . .
>
> He spoke; I surrendered. He talked us down, intelligent and foolish, man and woman, old and young. He never came to an end, for a quarter of an hour, for a half-hour, for three, four hours, always the same, never anything else; eternally in a circle he bored until he reached into the depths. He repeated his message not seven times but seventy-seven, and yet he was not satisfied.
>
> After a quarter of an hour he was dripping wet; his collar stuck to him like a wet rag at his throat, the veins were swollen in his forehead, he shuddered as in a fever, he threatened with widespread gestures, he enticed us, he exorcised us. He had thrown the lock of hair over his forehead, and still he did not stop, and no one wanted it to end. Everyone trembled in expectation of something monstrous, and I noticed with a shudder that I trembled like everyone else and that I had become only one atom in the total mass. . . .
>
> I noticed on the faces around me, in the tense, disturbed features, in the trembling limbs, that the climax had not yet been reached but that it had to come in the next few seconds. After a monstrous, unfathomable outburst of hate against the Marxist brood of Jews, it came over him and over us. It was the moment when the orator with his hoarse voice, his Austrian accent, suddenly lost himself—German blood! German blood! German blood! he screamed—some did not know whether it was out of love for this blood or out of fear for this divine blood. Did he himself know? He spoke in tongues. It overcame him, it overcame us; and we were no longer what we had been before. . . . It sprang from person to person, three thousand became one soul. From above to below, from one corner of the room to the other. Irresistible, with lightning speed, a monstrous cataract, the elemental set free. He no longer stood above us on the rudely built podium, he was next to us, in us, he burrowed around in the innermost recesses, and he crushed us with his servile lust for success to obey, to obliterate oneself, to be beneath, to be nothing. . . . He sobbed, he screamed; something inexplicable, primi-

tive, naked, bloody, burst in gushes from him; he could not stop it. There were no more sentences, no more articulated words; the satanic soul which was always hidden had pushed to the surface and no one could withstand it. Germany! Germany! Germany!

There are large stretches of *The Eyewitness* that are less compelling than what has just been described, and, especially in its romantic and melancholy strains, the novel is decidedly an imitative and minor work. Nevertheless, at its best it does present the challenge of a serious mind pondering some serious matter, and it succeeds, at least intermittently, in showing what it must have been like to stand in blind adoration of Hitler's will.

The importance of *The Eyewitness*, then, is that it keeps alive at least two questions that have been with us from the start but are still to be answered satisfactorily: How did this unknown Austrian soldier emerge from an impoverished and generally abject, knockabout existence to the heights of political power in Europe? And how did he come to command such an immense and passionately devoted following? In the last analysis, fiction may not be the best medium for answering these questions, but at its most vividly drawn it can effectively raise them and make them real for us. In the high moments of his novel, Ernst Weiss came close to doing that.

Beryl Bainbridge, the English novelist, looked back to what she believed to be a still earlier episode in Hitler's life for her *Young Adolf* (1979). Bainbridge is a much more accomplished writer than Weiss was and produced a subtler, more consistently refined and successfully managed novel; yet as a piece of historical fiction *Young Adolf* is seriously handicapped by the author's reliance on a highly questionable and almost certainly bogus source—*The Memoirs of Bridget Hitler*. Purportedly written by the Irish wife of Hitler's half brother Alois, these "memoirs" have been discounted as spurious by virtually every reputable scholar who has examined them. A little fiction in themselves, they attempt to fill in a "lost year" in Hitler's biography by having the young Adolf on a visit to his relatives in Liverpool (where Alois Hitler did, in fact, live for a time). There is nothing in any of the known historical sources to confirm such a visit, and the whole episode, as recounted in Bridget Hitler's "memoirs," is full of errors about Hitler's early life and shows all the signs of being an invention. Nevertheless, Beryl Bainbridge, who is herself from Liverpool and who was obviously tantalized by the notion that her native city once played host to the young Hitler, took *The Memoirs of Bridget Hitler* as creditable fact and used them as the basis for her book about "Hitler in Liverpool."

What is one to make of *Young Adolf*? Since the episode recounted at the heart of the novel is a fabrication, the book obviously does not hold up as a piece of historical fiction. That is not to say, though, that it cannot be read apart from its sources and judged as a fiction in its own terms. What, then, does *Young Adolf* look like when cut loose from *The Memoirs of Bridget Hitler*?

As the novel begins, young Adolf is twenty-three years old and on the lam from the Austrian authorities, who want to conscript him into the army. The year is 1912, a good time for someone with no taste for military service to be out of the country. Friendless and penniless, he goes to Liverpool, where his half brother Alois, a waiter and a razor-blade sales-man, lives with his Irish wife, Bridget, and baby son, "darling Pat." The young Adolf is a bother to everyone concerned, proves to be clumsy, lazy, and generally incompetent, and spends his days lying around and won-dering what to do. His brother dislikes him and occasionally knocks him about; his sister-in-law finds him an inconvenience and wants him gone. Life is petty, hostile in innumerable small ways, and holds little promise for anyone unfortunate enough to inhabit the cramped and crowded spaces of lower-class Liverpool. Nobody counts for very much in the present, including the feckless and all-too-foreign Adolphus, and in the end his exasperated English relatives buy his return ticket and send him packing into a future that seems equally bleak and without promise. Adolf curses them all from the window of his departing train, and they con-clude, in the novel's single memorable line, "Such a strong-willed young man. It is a pity he will never amount to anything."

Bainbridge is a fine writer and develops her fictional world of small, sad oppressions with great skill. There is no faulting her abilities to control her narrative completely and to fill it with an abundance of vivid, local detail. She is a strongly visual writer, and one has no difficulty whatever entering her Liverpool. Still, the question remains, why did she put the youthful Hitler in an English setting? What does he look like there, and how are readers likely to respond to him?

Two portraits of young Adolf emerge from the novel, and doubtless evoke at least two different responses. On the one hand, it is clear that he is lazy, dishonest, ill-tempered, astounded, absurd; he is also gawky, slovenly, clumsy, altogether lacking in charm, talent, and any other means to win his way in the world; in sum, he is pretty much a bum. At the same time, and while not denying the negative character traits just mentioned, he is shown in a somewhat more sympathetic light, as the largely passive and pathetic victim of his social circumstances and other people's acts of unkindness and aggression. He is hungry, threadbare, too often miserable for a young man; he is also unlucky and unloved, a down-and-out loner who needs to be taken in and cared for, lest all human feeling for the unfortunate be lost; he is, therefore, someone to be received with pity and at least a measure of civil kindness. In part, he is the type of the *schlemiel*—when he goes out, it rains; when he puts on his hat, the wind blows and carries it away; when he sits down, the chair moves out from under him and sends him tumbling under the table. Comic pratfalls accompany his every other move, and, in the view of at least one reviewer, he is, as a result, "wildly, broadly funny" and embodies "gallows humor at its most extreme." Others find "something likable about his continued hope for his own small life in the face of a world that despises him" and see "something dignified in his self-regard." Following this line of feeling, the reviewer for *Atlantic* noted that "one begins to think of him as 'young Adolf' rather than as 'Hitler,'" and, in the natural extension of this view, still another reviewer concluded that "*Young Adolf* is so well imagined and so completely imaginary that it's actually possible to feel sympathy for someone named Hitler."

The dust jacket of the American edition of Bainbridge's novel features a photograph of Adolf Hitler in brown shirt; the eyes that stare out of this face are the hard and menacing eyes of the Führer, not of some hapless youth. In *Young Adolf* itself, though, there is not a hint of menace, indeed hardly a hint of the future at all. Apart from the fact that Bainbridge's awkward hero comes to own a brown shirt, envisions himself with a mustache, and combs his hair over one eye, there is almost no link with what is to come in the years ahead. The novel turns around a moment of time that has its own minor troubles and preoccupations, its own muted sufferings, and is oblivious to anything larger and more monstrous that the future may hold. Indeed, had the author called her central character Hans or Fritz, there would be little compulsion to take any interest in him at all, and his story would be passed over as pretty much of a bore. As is, though, one reads *Young Adolf* with one eye on the novel, the other on history, and "completes" the narrative, so to speak, knowing full well that the small irony at its close ("It is a pity he will never amount to anything") will be amplified many times over and in the harshest way as a consequence of events outside the novel. Nothing of that coming terror can be glimpsed in the pages of *Young Adolf,* though, which instead serve to personalize and to humanize Hitler and to win for him a measure of sympathy and pity far greater than Adolf once grown up was ever to show to the peoples of Europe.

The most ambitious attempt to date to fictionalize Hitler in light of the historical record is Richard Hughes's projected multivolume work, "The Human Predicament." Conceived "as a long historical novel of my own times culminating in the Second World War," the project was left incomplete at the author's death in 1976. The two volumes that did appear, *The Fox in the Attic* (1961) and *The Wooden Shepherdess* (1973), however, stand by themselves as separate novels and indicate the major lines of the task that Hughes had set for himself. The critical reception of both novels was highly favorable, with more than one reviewer praising the "Tolstoian" scope of Hughes's undertaking and hailing his fiction as "an undoubted masterpiece" and "one of the major novels of our time." At the same time, and looked at from the standpoint of present concerns, both novels are also seriously flawed and show the difficulties confronting any writer who sets out to portray in fiction so massive a historical presence as Hitler.

Given the size of the author's conception and the unusually broad canvas of characters, places, and events he has drawn, it is not easy to summarize conveniently either *The Fox in the Attic* or *The Wooden Shepherdess.* The protagonist of both books is Augustine Penry-Herbert, a young, good-natured, but generally naive and unenlightened Englishman, who is carried through a series of personal and political awakenings that never quite bring him to full maturity. The major action of the first novel takes place in October–November 1923, and is set in Great Britain and Germany; its sequel advances the historical calendar to 1934 and takes young Augustine across several continents, beginning in the United States but also including a series of adventures in Paris, Germany, South Wales, and Morocco. Given the total thrust of "The Human Predicament," it is clear that Hughes had set out to write far more than still another English *Bildungsroman* and was aiming at something closer to *War and Peace*—a huge fictional history of the crucial decades of the twentieth century, replete with significant reference to the major figures and events of the day and sustained reflection on the impact of these on a representative consciousness of the times. The action would carry Augustine through all the personal trials of familial, romantic intellectual, artistic, religious, and political encounter but would do so in such a way as to transcend the limitations of merely subjective experience and offer some substantial analysis of the tenor of the times. The largest subject of "The Human Predicament, " in other words, would be the moral and political character of Western civilization as it played itself out against the backdrop of events in Europe in the decades between the two world wars.

Given this intention, one can see readily enough why Richard Hughes became fascinated by Adolf Hitler and wanted to include him in his fictional world. In art as in love, though, desire is one thing, execution another, and while the wish to represent Hitler as a key player in the turmoil of the twenties and thirties is understandable, the portraits themselves presented the author with problems he was unable to wholly solve.

In *The Fox in the Attic*, for instance, Hitler is not introduced until page 190 and occupies less than fifty pages of a 350-page narrative, which is to say that he is no more than an interlude among characters and actions of various sorts. The novel is deeply involved with pondering problems of personality, politics, and religion and finds its unity of reflection, if at all, in meditations upon two sharply contrasting psychological types—the "I" of the mystic, which effaces the primacy of selfhood and dissolves subjectivity in perceptions of the divine, and the "I" of the solipsist, which knows no "other" at all and treats every manifestation of separateness as a threat to be overcome by aggressive assertions of the self. Hughes intermittently incorporated little reflective essays on Freud and personality theory into his fiction, and *The Fox in the Attic* really does sound at times as abstractly theoretical and schematic as what has just been described above. Within this scheme, Hitler is made to portray the type of the solipsist, and Mitzi, one of Augustine's Bavarian cousins, who is stricken with blindness and, at novel's end, enters a convent to assume a religious vocation, embodies the type of the mystic. The contrast is not without its interest, but it is drawn in far too obvious and explicit a way to succeed as fiction, and in any case hardly requires an Adolf Hitler to illustrate it. Given the preponderant weight of the man in history, his appearance in this kind of psychological allegory seems unbalanced and badly misplaced.

Hughes succeeds better when he attempts something closer to straight historical exposition, although even here one wonders if the gains in representation significantly outweigh the losses. The Hitler of *The Fox in the Attic* is the Hitler of the Munich beer hall putsch of November 1923, which is to say, a failed Hitler. Hughes worked chiefly from well-known historical works (he lists these by name in an author's acknowledgments page) and, in portraying the abortive take-over, rarely strays from them. Hitler, Göring, Röhm, Kahr, Ludendorff, and Hanfstängl are all here, dramatized beyond their appearances in most strictly historical accounts of the putsch but otherwise recognizable in their respective roles. In its broad lines, the scene is generally well done, but it conveys to the reader neither more nor less than he would get from Bullock, Toland, Fest, or any of the other standard biographical accounts. That being the case, the question is why fictionalize Hitler at all, and how fictionalize him in a way that will render him more understandable than otherwise would be the case?

In reading *The Fox in the Attic* one gets the sense that these are questions that Hughes failed to think through adequately enough. He was interested in Hitler as an exemplar of what he took to be the larger forces of the day, especially those rooted in moral and political anarchy, but otherwise he did not see him in very sustained or even very clear historical focus. Psychology and not history drew him, and he was more intent in fleshing out Hitler as the quintessential solipsist than as the political and national leader that Hitler was grooming himself to become. Beyond that, Hughes was interested in getting under the skin of the man to touch the nerve of his feelings, especially his feelings of personal ambition, frustration, and pain. Thus there are passages that touch on the tenderness of family sentiment (Hitler is portrayed as being good with other people's children), on erotic repression (his ogling but avoidance of the Viennese whores), on his fear and hatred of Jews (but just in passing, as if his antisemitism were an incidental and not an essential part of his character). There are also passages on his performances as an orator, but these are relatively few and do not measure up to the much fuller and more vividly drawn descriptions of Hitler's oratory in *The Eyewitness*. Finally, and perhaps most graphically, there are extended passages on Hitler in physical pain (he badly injured a shoulder escaping the Munich police following the beer hall putsch), passages that begin to engage the sympathies of any feeling person conscious of another's agony:

> . . . the man looked half fainting: for the moment the one thing he needed above all else was a bed. So she told his two friends to take him away upstairs.
>
> Hitler went up with them docilely, in a miserable daze. . . . But not to bed! For once they had got him alone up there they stretched him out on the floor and knelt on him. One was a doctor, and they wrestled again and again with that dislocated shoulder to get it back into joint. They had no anaesthetics and for a long time and even downstairs and with the doors shut Helene could hear him: while the frightened baby woke and wailed.
>
> But it was all too inflamed by now to discover that as well as the dislocation the collarbone was broken; and so, for all the doctor's skill, they failed—and finally they gave it up and left him. . . .
>
> Hitler had been already half delirious with pain and frustration when he arrived: now he was growing more feverish still. The torn and twisted sinews were shrinking, the broken bone grated, and pain was piled on pain. If only Putzi had been there to play Wagner to him, as David's harp soothed Saul!

A reader who did not previously know that the ailing Hitler hid away for two days in the attic of Putzi Hanfstängl's summer cottage in Uffing, outside Munich, will learn as much from this episode of *The Fox in the Attic*. Such a reader will doubtless also get some idea of how painful a broken collarbone can be and probably will respond in sympathy to the person who suffers so. Until, that is, he realizes that the poor unfortunate is named Hitler, at which point he will either willfully withdraw sympathy or suffer a number of confused and conflicting feelings himself. This dissonance of affect is awakened elsewhere in the novel and is, in fact, an inevitable accompaniment of any fiction about Hitler that brings the man down to human scale and portrays him as someone who suffered as well as perpetrated an excess of pain. One unavoidable aspect of representing Hitler in such terms at all, therefore, is that one returns him to the human family he set out to destroy and makes him a recipient of the whole range of human feelings, including, as in this case, the more benevolent feelings of sympathetic caring.

This problem probably would not arise, or at least would not arise so acutely, if historical novels about Hitler would portray the man against the entirety of his career, including his responsibility for the years of mass destruction. No matter what the range of his personal sorrows, if one sees him within the context of the continent-wide terror he brought on, there is little likelihood that reader's feelings would be drawn in the manner described above. The fact is, though, that most historical fiction about Hitler is selective in its focus and searches out one or two episodes in the life, and usually the early ones at that. Thus, while *The Wooden Shepherdess* continues to chronicle the growth of the Nazi movement, it does not yet reach the period of the Nazi conquests and the horrors that accompanied them across Europe. Rather, it carries Augustine back and forth across the seas, introduces him to new levels of sexual and political experience, follows Mitzi through the various stages of religious enlightenment, and continues to describe Hitler's quest for political power. Apart, though, from noting Hughes's lingering fascination with questions of radical ego dissolution and assertion, as represented once more by the divergent personalities of Mitzi and Hitler, it is difficult to see what unites these different narrative strands and gives coherence to the novel.

Like its predecessor, *The Wooden Shepherdess* is intellectually ambitious and clearly dedicated to saying something significant about the character of European life in the years leading up to the Second World War. There is a diverse array of fictional characters present, a dense accumulation of historical detail, and numerous authorial asides that attempt to articulate a philosophy of history. Just what the novel as a whole adds up to and how the episodes involving Hitler are intended to contribute to its overall meaning, however, remains uncertain.

Hitler is first introduced on page 145, and hence is once more a late and only occasional presence in the narrative. In the aftermath of his arrest following the putsch, he is briefly glimpsed in Landsberg prison, where he wrote *Mein Kampf.* The scenes that follow describe his trial, his release, his climb to power amidst the dissolution of the Weimar Republic. Göring, Goebbels, Hess, Strasser, Speer, Himmler, Hanfstängl, and Röhm are all alluded to as allies or enemies, and one begins to get the

sense of intraparty rivalry and intrigue; however, no one but Hitler among
the major Nazis begins to stand out as a character in his own right, and
even Hitler is described mostly from without, as a ready-made rather
than as a fictionally realized presence. On those relatively few occasions
when he is given the chance to speak in his own person the dialogue is
artificial and tends to sound simpleminded: "But where have you hidden
your new baby sister, you rascal?" Hitler, as "Onkel Dolf," says to a four-
year-old child; and to his host, while enjoying an elegant dinner, "Hanfstängl, you are quite the most upper-class person I know!" (It is a characteristic of almost all of the fiction about Hitler that the only manner of his
speech that is rendered credibly is diatribe, the overheated style of his
platform oratory; otherwise, fiction writers have hardly been able to imagine the man speaking at all.)

For most of his time in the novel Hitler is described plotting his "Blood
Purge" of Röhm and the S.A., an action that culminated on June 30, 1934,
in the infamous "Night of the Long Knives." Unlike the author's earlier
description of the beer hall putsch, for which he could rely on well-
established historical accounts, Hughes was moved to more freely invent
the "Blood Purge" (the official records did not survive the war and probably were destroyed by the Nazis themselves), but his reconstruction is in
line with what is generally known about the killings. The elimination of
Röhm and his strong-arm boys was an important moment in Hitler's early
career, for it did away with the possibility of another armed gang seizing
power in Germany. Hughes brings the event to fictional life by dramatiz-
ing the sordid details of the murders and does so in a way that extends the
note of Gothic horror that began to make itself felt in the previous novel.
In this respect *The Wooden Shepherdess,* like *The Fox in the Attic,* weds
historical fiction to some of the well-established conventions of popular
novels of suspense and intrigue and points a direction that later and more
blatantly commercial writers will follow with a vengeance. The terror
introduced in *The Wooden Shepherdess* is not grossly exploited for its own
sake, however, and, following the scenes that describe the "Blood Purge,"
Hughes returns to more commonplace reflections on politics and ends his
novel with Mitzi in her Carmelite cell struggling between presentiments
of Satan loose across the land and the overwhelming advent of God.

Had the author lived to complete "The Human Predicament" (it would
have necessitated at least a trilogy), it would be easier than it is now to

understand just what he intended by juxtaposing his historical fiction on Hitler and the rise of Nazism with his meditative fiction on Mitzi and mystical Christianity. Augustine, never a very strong presence to begin with, becomes weaker as the novels progress and by the end of *The Wooden Shepherdess* has virtually disappeared from the narrative altogether. One is left, therefore, with a vision of Europe caught between the oppositions of a brutal and megalomaniacal politics and the sanctity of ecstatic faith, an opposition that history itself was to resolve during World War II with the virtual destruction of both.

What is missing from Hughes's novels, as indeed from most other attempts to write historical fiction about Hitler, are the very things for which the leader of the Third Reich is remembered today. There are no references to the ghettos and extermination camps, and hardly even a hint of the anti-Jewish persecutions that preceded them. The same is by and large true in the novels of Weiss and Bainbridge, both of which present a Hitler without victims. The specific evils that we associate with Nazism are absent, in fact, from all of these books, an absence that greatly limits their effectiveness and impact as historically informed fictions. To be sure, the reader knows more about Hitler and his crimes than a given author may be willing to tell him in any single book, and much of the irony of these fictions is a result of the writer's manipulation of such foreknowledge. When, for instance, Hughes writes that, in the aftermath of World War I, it was an absolute belief in England that "never till the end of Time could there be another war," and then proceeds to develop the beginnings of the rise of Hitler, it is clear that he is writing as an ironist. It is a weak irony, however, and fails to evoke the element of moral shock that should be triggered by the spectacle of Europe beset by an insurgent Nazism. Likewise, Beryl Bainbridge can hardly move us beyond a brief snicker of contrary knowledge when, at the end of her novel, she sends young Adolf back to Germany with the offhand remark that he will probably not amount to very much. In both cases, the discordant note of ironic awareness registers, but it does so without significant impact and for most readers will not carry beyond the moment of its sounding.

The failure of these fictions, therefore, is owing to their inability to achieve a lasting moral resonance, itself the consequence of limiting artistic representation to only a narrow and naturalistically conceived slice of history. Put another way, the Hitler one encounters in these books—the

Hitler of Pasewalk, of an apocryphal visit to Liverpool, of the Munich beer hall putsch and the "Blood Purge"—is not yet the Hitler of apocalyptic history, the driven and demonic leader of the Nazi furies. He does not sustain interest because he does not yet symbolize anything larger than himself, and the particular moment in time in which he is glimpsed by Weiss, Bainbridge, and Hughes, while not without its own fascination, does not carry very far beyond itself. It would take another kind of fiction to develop those extensions beyond historical time, one whose preoccupation is less with the claims of factuality than with the collective fears and desires of fantasy life, a fiction that would appeal to contemporary tastes for the horrid, the lurid, the most monstrous of human shapes imaginable. In a word, it would take the thriller, the literary form that sustains our taste for crime and turns it into popular entertainment.

IV

The Fascination of Abomination

"I am the expression of your most
secret desires."

—ADOLF HITLER, in Hans-Jürgen
Syberberg's *Hitler, A Film from
Germany*

OPENING LINES, as every writer of popular fiction knows, are the most important in the book, for if you cannot draw a reader's interest on page one, it is unlikely he will still be with you by page two. For this reason, writers will summon up all the ingenuity they can muster to start off with something seductively novel, alluring, simply irresistible:

> At the age of seventy there is something intensely pleasurable in having a naked girl walk across the small of one's back. At all events, that was the view of Norman Cavendish, who, being seventy and having at that moment a young woman performing that function, felt that he was in a position to know.
> 'Gabrielle—a little more over the shoulders, please. . . .'
> 'Is that all right?'
> 'Marvellous, my dear.'
> The toes danced on the flesh. . . .

So begins Richard Hugo's *The Hitler Diaries,* a recent thriller about "the most evil man the world has ever known: Adolf Hitler." According to the back-cover blurb (the opener before the opener; together with the front-cover picture, the true tease into the innards of a book), the novel will bring the reader into a world of "power, politics, pornography, and mania." Together with the power and glamour that attach to "money," these are the "big four" of commercial fiction, and most books aiming to achieve best-sellerdom will manipulate them in one combination or another. For an adventure thriller to truly stand out, therefore, something more is needed, some dimension of desire or fear not usually addressed in run-of-the-mill fiction. To get in this extra angle, Hugo and his publishers did what so many others are now doing as well—they popped the historical question, "the ultimate question of World War II: *who left the Berlin bunker alive?*"

The Hitler Diaries won't tell us, of course, at least won't tell anything that historians have not already told us over the last forty years, but that is not the point. What is, is that the question itself is still around, still open and somehow capable of stimulating new theories about mistaken identities, last-minute escapes, substitute corpses, miraculous rescues. After all the hoaxes, all the forgeries, all the false sightings and counter-historical fictions, something keeps before us the impossible question: *Where is Hitler?*

It cannot be answered historically, this question which is no question, but that is not to say that it cannot be answered at all. Whether imagined in his bunker or out of his bunker, Hitler is today all around us—in our loathing, our fears, our fantasies of power and victimization, our nightmares of vile experience and violent endings. All of which is to say that he has surfaced as a dark presence in the turbulent underside of our dreams and is increasingly to be found in precisely those fictions that are about "power, politics, pornography, and mania." He is, in fact, the ultimate test of the affective potency of such fictions, the measure of their capacity to mirror if not to match the historical example of extremity he set.

"Think of the most frightening thing that can be," reads an apposite line from *The Asgard Solution,* and you will have found Hitler. Because he has taken up residency in some of our deepest apprehensions and stands today as the incarnation of our wildest and most fearful imaginings, he has become a convenient touchstone for writers of suspense and horror fiction, who know that merely to evoke his name is readily to garner sensations of a horrific sort. It might all be passed off as a lot of fun if it did not contribute to the contamination of historical memory or incite the fantasy levels of those who would still like to live within the terms of the Nazi dream.

This dream, in Hugo's version of it, remains with Norman Cavendish and his poolside playmate only long enough to introduce some kinky sex into the novel, after which the sporty septuagenarian and his lovely nymphet are violently dispatched by a team of hired killers. Thereafter, the narrative gets down to more serious business—business said to be worth tens of millions and capable of sending into action American, Soviet, and Israeli intelligence agents, business that multiplies corpses and love affairs in about equal number and posits a future ruled over by a Nazi cabal. In a word, the Hitler business.

Most people presumably know it's all a put-on but keep on reading anyway, not, in the first place, to learn anything substantially new about history, but rather for the sheer excitement of vicariously reliving the story of history's worst crime. Thrillers are a kind of literary dope and tend to make addicts out of their readers. When the addiction is fed by the promise of "extra" sensations held out by the symbolism of the Nazi era, the temperature of readers' expectations suddenly shoots upward several degrees.

The reaction is more than a little perverse, for given all we know about Hitler and the horrors he brought on, one would think that images of the man would repel, not attract. Yet a large public is drawn by the prospect of being let into latter-day revelations, no matter how fanciful, about the Third Reich and its infamous Führer. Project these fictions as if they somehow touched on fact—*could* have happened, *might* have been true—and it hardly matters at all that they are made up. Thus *The Climate of Hell* advertises itself as "a fiction based on fact"; *The Asgard Solution* as "a work of fiction [that] could have been fact"; *The Man Who Killed Hitler* as a composite of the real and the imagined that invites the reader himself to determine "how much is true." "That," the book declares, "is for you to decide."

With this kind of open-ended invitation to fantasy, a whole host of questions rushes to mind, any one of which is capable of giving birth to bizarre new speculations about Hitler. Did he really die in the bunker? Is it true that he left behind a son? Are there surviving letters or diaries that will at last unlock the secret nature of the man and his ambition? Was he tender or cruel with Eva Braun? Are his followers today planning to establish a Fourth Reich to rule the world according to his ideas? The corpus of pseudohistorical fiction accumulates around these questions as women do around James Bond and, in a simpleminded but apparently successful way, manages to keep alive the desire to ask, still one more time, "What more would you know about Adolf Hitler?"

Would you, for instance, like to know more about his erotic side? (An unsubtle, unworthy question, yet a persistent one.) The historical fiction knows almost nothing of it and hardly hints at passions other than those of megalomania. As for historical scholarship, it speculates variously about Hitler's sexual inclinations, asserting both that he was normal (as in the studies by Toland and Maser) and that he indulged in the grossest of sexual perversions (Waite). To the popular fantasists it hardly matters what the historians say, though, for their fictions are written to satisfy other desires than the wish for veracity and do not pretend to rest on biographical evidence.

The major sex scene in *The Hitler Diaries*, for example, is straight pornokitsch, projecting as it does an Eva Braun who works herself up slavishly before her amazed and disgusted lover only to find that he has more self-centered pleasures in mind and will give her nothing but his scorn. The Hitler portrayed here (supposedly from his own "secret" diaries) is anything but normal and subjects the begging Eva to sexual humiliation, deprivation, and abuse. The point, if there is one, is to show Hitler as conqueror and denier of woman and to expose Eva, the primal woman, as Eve—"Mother of downfall! Drainer of virtue and strength!" It's all pretty hysterical and degrading but over and done with in a few pages, after which the novel proceeds to chart a world that is generally free of femaleness, preoccupied as it is instead with the masculine pleasures of sleuthing, moneymaking, and murder.

Other fictions vary the image only slightly, paying token attention to sexual pursuits and remaining mostly within a male world of fast-paced action and adventure. The popular image of Hitler, in other words, does not lend itself very well to prolonged sexual fantasy unless sex is in the service of exaggerated ego-power (as, of course, it often is). An early fiction entitled *Hitler's Wife* dreams up a pre–World War I marriage between Hitler and Eva Braun in order to show that Hitler's adventures in love are parallel to those in the realm of politics. Eva, or "Evi," as she is called in the novel, cuckolds her husband, who is portrayed as being authoritarian, awkward, and sexually incapable. The novel suggests that this early episode of marital defilement was to influence decisively Hitler's later political career, but the narrative, which was published during the war years, undoubtedly as a piece of anti-Nazi propaganda, is so poorly conceived and so wretchedly written that few would have believed it in its day and even fewer would find any reason to read it today.

Gus Weill's *The Führer Seed,* an exploitative novel published more recently, presents a more macho image of Hitler, or at least of Hitler's "seed." A fiction in the mode of *The Boys from Brazil* and other books that posit the existence of a Hitler progeny, *The Führer Seed* links neo-Nazis with Colonel Qadaffi in a plot to take over the world. Hitler himself is long since gone, but the spirit of "the most evil man who ever lived" is around to preside over the doings of his "son," Kurt Hitler, the governing mayor of West Berlin, including his bedroom doings. The sex scenes, which bring together this latter-day Hitler with Diane Abramson, the perverse and sexually insatiable widow of an enormously wealthy Jew, include fellatio and anal intercourse as well as conventional sex and symbolically link extreme eroticism with money, power, and political ambition, all to forge a union of ultimate and unmatched potency. The Hitler element in all of this is its dimension of excess ("It's who you are [the son of Hitler] that turns me on!" whispers the Wild Widow Abramson to her soon-to-be-depleted lover), but it is difficult to sustain the image of Hitler as sexual stud, and, after some intermittent indulgences of the pornographic imagination, the novel settles into a conventional thriller plot and spins a tale of international intrigue not unlike that to be found in dozens of other cheap novels.

Roland Puccetti's *The Death of the Führer* goes it one better in invention by creating one of the more novel versions of Hitler to be found in popular literature. Using a quotation from *The Last Days of Hitler* as an inscription, the book turns tables on Trevor-Roper and sets out to develop a counter-historical fiction in which Hitler survives his own death through a last-minute brain extraction by Nazi scientists in the Berlin bunker. The brain is then transplanted into another person, who becomes the new Führer and who will keep alive the hope of world conquest by a revived German Reich. The question that antifascist fighters of this scheme must answer, then, is: Who is the new Hitler? Can he be found and destroyed before the "sleeping Reich" awakens and once more brings destruction across the earth?

The motif of Frankenstein's monster is complexly refashioned in *The*

Death of the Führer, a novel that combines its special effects of terror and suspense with strong elements of science fiction and sadistic sexuality. Play these off against the backdrop of a neo-Nazi revival and place them within the context of an intricately plotted medical thriller and you have quite a story.

It begins with the protagonist descending at night into the Führerbunker, a descent that mirrors the claustrophobic fantasies of some of Poe's best interment stories. Traces of an operation in a hidden room reveal that Hitler's brain was extracted while the Führer was still alive and could be functioning still today in another body. The search for the new Hitler carries the plot to Spain, where a sizable group of Nazis keeps alive the spirit of the Third Reich and plans its next moves. One of this group is Hitler himself, or at least the body that houses the brain of Hitler. But which one?

To find out, the protagonist, who manages to penetrate this cabal by passing himself off as an old-time SS officer, begins to court the one woman in the group in the hope that she may reveal to him the secret identity of the Führer. She is described in the conventional terms of the pornographic thriller—as gorgeous, sexy, and sex-starved—and is brought together with the male lead in a vividly described bedroom scene. At the very height of sexual climax, she unlocks for him the secret he is after by uttering, out of her passion, "ICH BIN DER FÜHRER." Whereupon he plunges a knife into her/him and has the satisfaction of crying out of his own moment of murderous exhilaration, "I had killed the Führer."

The novel doesn't end there, but everything that follows is anticlimactic given this culminating moment of sexual slaying. As in virtually all of these books, the avenging knife is wielded by a Jew (it is mandatory that at least one of his parents must have perished in Auschwitz), who fulfills the recurring fantasy of Nazi-Jewish copulation, which is by now pretty much a commonplace in the literature. The idea of the Jew coupling with a Hitler refashioned as a female, in a novel that elsewhere alludes to sordid homosexual and sadomasochistic sex, extends the fantasy in an especially loathsome way, but by its very extremity begins to reveal something of the perverse appeal of much of the Hitler literature.

It is an appeal that invariably reduces women to objects of sexual violence and men to erotic gangsters and cruelly impassioned killers. The common element in both types is sexual bestiality, which is portrayed in its most exaggerated forms whenever the Jew is brought into the picture. The exploitation of the feminine is then at its most complete. As a result of popular fascination with the workings of the Nazi concentration camp system, a whole new vocabulary of sexual enslavement is now available to the pornographic imagination and is freely appropriated in both the common run of smut literature as well as in more sophisticated fiction about female victimization. Newsreels and other documentaries from World War II have made graphically visual the ordeals that Jewish women were forced to undergo by the Nazis and their allies, and these pictures once seen seem to settle in the dark underside of imagination and have the capacity to trigger erotic fantasies of the most perverse kind. They have come to define the furthest limits of human cruelty in the pulps and, beyond that, now stand behind every anticipated enactment of sexual ravishment in a mass-sadistic sense. To be sure, there are and always have been other forms of sexual brutality, but the imagination of *total* sexual degradation today is Nazi-inspired and comes to us from the barbarism carried out in the ghettos and concentration camps. If there is such a thing as sexual memory, then, the experience of countless Jewish women in these hellish places stands at the center of it, as it does of much of the corpus of sexually exploitative fiction.

As for Jewish men, they have hardly fared much better. In book after book, the Jew is portrayed as an obsessive, vengeful killer, one who will stop at nothing until his aim of destroying his enemy has been achieved. In recognizing this role for what it is, one begins to see that in its cumulative effects, if not necessarily in its basic intentions, popular fiction that invokes Hitler or otherwise draws extensively upon Nazi symbolism tends to revive some of the oldest and most persistent of antisemitic fantasies. In its classic expression, the nightmare pictures the Jew as assassin and portrays him knife in hand standing before a terrified Christian woman or child. As he previously slew the Christian Lord, so now he will draw the blood of the lady and/or innocent babe. By nature a vicious predator who regards the whole world with hostility and, with his coreligionists is engaged in a sinister plot to take it over, the Jew is nothing less than the Primal Enemy of mankind and in numerous insidious ways is embarked on a campaign of world conquest.

In simple terms, this is the myth set forth in the notorious *Protocols of the Elders of Zion* and, with its sexual aspect heightened and made more graphically horrific, in the racist cartoons of Streicher's *Der Stürmer*. Hitler was obsessed with this spectre of the Jew and exploited it repeatedly in his writings and talk. It allowed him to justify his anti-Jewish program on the grounds of "self-defense," as a preemptive purging of the Jew before the contaminator and killer of mankind could complete his evil schemes. Thus the Nazis believed they had a popular mandate, based on centuries-old antisemitic fears, to slay the slayer in their midst.

Following the mass slaughter of Jews during World War II, these disgraceful notions seemed to disappear—one would have hoped, for good. The hope has been proven naive, however, for while it may no longer be respectable to profess antisemitic ideas openly, the feelings and fears that underlay these ideas have hardly disappeared. Rather, they went underground and of late have resurfaced in a variety of forms, including the literary forms being looked at here. To be sure, none of these books specifically aims to revive Hitlerian antisemitism, but it lies in the nature of their preoccupations with Hitler to reawaken the terms of the ancient anti-Jewish animus, even if time and again in inverted or otherwise disguised form.

The enemies this time are not the Christian innocents but the Nazis, and it is entirely acceptable within the conventions of thriller fiction to justify aggression against them. Since everyone knows that they are the ones who previously hunted down and destroyed the Jews, it is alright this time around for the Jews to get in their licks against them. In the pursuit of the hunter by the erstwhile hunted, though, it is easy to confuse who is who, and it comes as no surprise to see that the Nazi-Jewish doppelgänger has by now become a familiar type in the literature. Thus Kurt Hitler, in *The Führer Seed,* can cry out to the Jew who is stalking him, "You could say I'm a Jew. Am I not being hounded, murdered, not for what I've done but for who I am? Isn't that the story of the Jewish people? Guilty because you are Jews?" Max Levy, a survivor of father Hitler's death camps and soon to be Kurt Hitler's assassin, will have none of it, though, and, in typical hardhearted way, shows the pleading young Hitler no mercy: "I am a victim of that ethnic disease, you hear it called the 'holocaust mentality.' I believe with all my heart and everything in me that if we do not kill them first, they will kill us." As here, Levy's heart is frozen through the whole book; in contrast to Kurt Hitler, who is portrayed as a swinger, the Jew is unable to love, either physically or spiritually. The incarnation of an old/new stereotype, his passion is concentrated single-mindedly on vengeance, and he will show no quarter to the young, good-looking, vital Nazi. "Israeli," Kurt Hitler addresses him, "wasn't Eichmann enough? Won't one monster suffice?" It won't, not for the merciless Jew, and Max Levy, deaf to the young man's pleas, does away with him without any further ado.

Other novels portray the Jew similarly, as a cunning, implacable killer, who resembles his Nazi quarry so closely as to appear at times his twin. In *Pursuit*, a thriller set mainly in Germany and Israel, Helmut von Schraeder, the "Monster of Maidanek," is made over by a plastic surgeon and emerges with a new identity—that of Benjamin Grossman, Israeli war hero. Physically, the SS man is now gone, but spiritually, so the fiction has it, he has cleverly disguised himself within the Jew, presumably the last place where one would look to locate the Nazi soul. It doesn't take much, however, to guess the outcome of the ruse, and before long it is clear that, while the face and the name may have changed, the lust for killing remains constant in von Schraeder/Grossman and, whether within Nazi or Jew, will be satisfied. The idea, to quote from the novel, is "that everyone in the world has a double somewhere, someone born the instant he was born, and who acted in every respect as he acted." Thus, according to this way of thinking, Nazi and Jew are interchangeable types, twin expressions of the same ruthless, imperishable urge to murder.

The point is reiterated at the close of Ira Levin's *The Boys from Brazil*, a popular thriller about the cloning of the Führer, in which the Jews are chastised for wanting to search out and destroy the little Hitlers. "People who would even kill children," so the simpleminded preachment goes, are doing "Mengele's business" and are no better than the Nazis themselves. The slide from moral virtue into instant debasement is presented as a quick and easy one for the Jew, who is warned in no uncertain terms to restrain his blood lust and to keep from what seems to be his natural inclination for infanticide: "Killing children, *any* children—it's wrong."

It's wrong to kill adults as well, yet at the end of *The Hitler Diaries*, a novel full of carnage, Max Weiss, the killer-Jew, waits in the shadows, gun in hand. In *The Climate of Hell*, another Mengele novel, the Jewish avenger is an Israeli psychopathic killer so dangerous that even the Mossad wants him put out of the way. And in *The Asgard Solution*, a thriller that mixes Nazis, Arabs, and Jews in every possible combination, the most impressive killer is the Jew Viktor Josef, who slays his enemies, including Adolf Hitler himself, in the most ingenious ways—employing at novel's end the most traditional of Jewish objects, a book (soaked in water and rolled up tightly to become an effective bludgeon).

What do all of these images of the Jew as aggressive, unstoppable killer add up to? The notion, repeated now in so much of popular fiction about Hitler and Hitlerism, is that the Jew, especially if portrayed as an Israeli, has adopted the mentality of his persecutor and mimics him in violent behavior. Moreover, it is not just that these Jews, afflicted as they are with the special characteristics of "holocaust mentality," go about murdering their enemies, but that they do so with such obvious pleasure. Read enough mass-market fiction and you will see soon enough that the Nazi credo of joy in violence has been revived in the post-Holocaust Jew.

The type was carried to the point of extravagant cliché in William Styron's best-selling novel *Sophie's Choice*, where in the character of Nathan Landau it becomes unambiguously clear that homicidal mania has been transferred from the Nazi to the Jew. Nathan, a composite of "the attractive and compelling" with "the subtly and indefinably sinister," recalls no one so much as Svengali, and abuses his blond and beautiful woman so constantly and with so much relish as to revive the wildest of antisemitic fantasies of the Jew as sexual predator. Inasmuch as Sophie is not only a Polish Catholic but a Holocaust survivor to boot, she stands as an especially poignant victim of the Jewish penchant for despoiling helpless Christian women and drives home the point that the demonic is now shared equally between the Nazi and the Jew. Especially when out of the depths of his perverse sexual cravings Nathan turns Sophie into Irma Griese, one of the monsters of Auschwitz, and makes her perform accordingly, he inevitably reawakens age-old fears of the carnal Jew and condemns poor Sophie to the company of countless ravaged heroines in antisemitic fiction. One would have thought the type was long since used up, but given the popular reception of Styron's novel and of the movie based upon it, that is obviously not the case.

What is the case, as one reconstructs it from *Sophie's Choice* and numerous other fictions that exploit the savage horrors of the Holocaust, is distressing and might be summed up by a single line from Styron's novel—"Oh, what ghoulish opportunism are writers prone to!" In book after book it is evident that the ghouls have been prowling out among the slaughter pits of Nazi-occupied Europe, and their prey is almost always the same: the helplessly attractive and hopelessly vulnerable Jewish woman. Readers of European novels have seen the type time and again. Sartre described her as well as anyone in his *Anti-Semite and Jew:*

> There is in the words "a beautiful Jewess" a very special sexual signification. . . . This phrase carries an aura of rape and massacre. The "beautiful Jewess" is she whom the Cossacks under the Czars dragged by her hair through the streets of her burning village. And the special works which are given over to accounts of flagellation reserve a place of honor for the Jewess. But it is not necessary to look into esoteric literature . . . the Jewess has a well-defined function in even the most serious novels. Frequently violated or beaten, she sometimes succeeds in escaping dishonor by means of death, but that is a form of justice.

Substitute "Nazis" for "Cossacks" in the above passage, and the description of the ravaged Jewess can fit much of the fiction under consideration here. What one sees in surveying it is the transposition of an old erotic type onto the new imaginative landscapes of slaughter: instead of burning villages, the fires of Auschwitz; but everything else, rape and massacre included, remains pretty much the same. Since the death camps heightened the spectre of sexual cruelty, though, the imaginative violation of the Jewish woman is generally intensified beyond its previous levels of fantasy, and the image of the Holocaust survivor as a new type of the desirable woman consequently seems that much more perverse.

Perverse or not, one finds her in books that range from serious novels by established authors to cheap porno thrillers written by pseudonymous hacks. The extent of her humiliation will vary within this range of writings, as will the description of the physical abuse to which she is subjected, but a common link among all is the inclination to portray the sexual desirability of the mutilated woman, a desirability closely akin in its passions to necrophilia. In subdued terms, that is one of the open secrets behind Philip Roth's transformation of Anne Frank as a post-Holocaust *femme fatale* in *The Ghost Writer,* as it is the chief motive behind the figure of Tamara in Isaac Bashevis Singer's mordant novel about Holocaust survivors, *Enemies, A Love Story.* The scarred lady of Bernard Malamud's "The Lady of the Lake" is a gentle version of the mutilated Jewess, as is Golda in André Schwarz-Bart's *The Last of the*

Just. To see her at her most explicitly drawn, though, one cannot do better than to observe in all of its repellent detail the obscenely memorable figure of Hannah in Herbert Gold's *My Last Two Thousand Years:*

> My name is Hannah. . . . Would you like to make love?
> She had a sly, sideways, welcoming smile in the slatted shadow of her first-class cabin. Rubbed mahogany, a table with a curved edge against tilting seas, a closet with mirror; and in the mirror, a girl was pulling a frock over her head. I didn't believe my eyes. I turned from the mirror to the girl. She slipped off her dress. I felt a swimming horror. . . .
> Her body was deformed, carved up, sculpted into a parody of an erotic demon. There were puckered lips, folds, crevices of flesh, scarred blinking receptacles, tightly pursed mouths, folded cicatrices which twisted like snakes when she moved.
> The thin and pretty face smiled at me. "It was an experiment they did," she said. "They had doctors, you know, I think? Who did these experiments. Anything a man could think of. You want? . . . Some men like."

This is strong stuff but not very much different in kind from descriptions of Sophie's wasted body in Styron's novel (her identification as a gentile, not a Jew, hardly matters here, for the type remains the same) or from some of the more revolting passages describing female victimization in Kosinski's *The Painted Bird.* The common element in all of these fictions is their development of an especially abhorrent pornography of violence, itself the germ of an emerging erotics of Auschwitz. The smut literature is full of it, but as the examples cited above indicate, one need not look to gutter pornography alone to find a fascination with fantasies of necrophiliac sex. The theme's fullest articulation to date, in fact, is to be found in a much-acclaimed novel by a highly respected writer—D. M. Thomas's *The White Hotel.*

Before considering the novel itself, one needs to pause at its cover design, for Thomas's publishers labored more diligently than most to give his book a graphic appeal that would immediately establish its note of deviant sexuality: the dust jacket features a naked woman with burning hair who is being literally consumed before our eyes by her strange passions. What is it that obsesses her so? The drawing on the hard-cover edition pictures her alone in a room, transfixed in an almost doll-like position in her rocking chair, hair ignited with flame, a solitary figure helplessly and almost complacently burning away. It is an image that one can neither easily forget nor easily explain.

The motif is carried over to the illustrated inside cover of the popular paperback edition, which features the same figure in a much fuller drawing. She is presented more sensually this time and occupies far more of the page; in fact, she takes up three different poses in what amounts to an erotic triptych. On the right-hand panel she sits as if in a hypnotic trance, her body bare and a bit tense, her eyes fixed strangely ahead, hands placed purposefully on her knees, hair crowned by fire. She is a figure of immobile passion, her nude form an upright pillar of unexpressed desire consumed by flame. She is not alone, although in her near-catatonic state she seems oblivious to the figure looking in at her through the window in the panel above.

The voyeur is a man, his demeanor hard, his posture stiff and menacing. In contrast to her soft, naked body, a study in white, he is fully dressed in dark grey military uniform, his head helmeted in steel, his hands holding a rifle with fixed bayonet. On his left arm there is a bright red military armband that shows a large black swastika in a field of white. The Nazi stares in at the lady, weapon in hand, but does not seem about to approach her. Rather, he is a blocking agent, his body on the ready against hers, his position an advantageous one, on guard against any move she might make. She is obviously a prisoner of his, as she is of her own strange passions, and she sits before him in her nakedness and burns and burns.

On the left-hand panel they are pictured together in bed, making love, he beginning to assume the upper position, she moving willingly beneath him. Her body is more relaxed and yielding, her hair no longer aflame. Lying on a bed of soft, white folds, they could be any couple caught in an embrace. One imagines that their love will be good.

In the panel immediately above their heads, though, a train is coming into view, its engine crowned by a puff of smoke that parallels the fire atop the lady's head in the right-hand panel. Tints of red accompany the otherwise dark form of the train and suggest a link with the red swastika armband. A group of five small, naked figures adjacent to the locomotive are in flight and represent a family in distress. Immediately adjacent to them is the armed Nazi soldier. And above his head and theirs, the lady appears a third time, her half-naked body caught in what could be a posture of love, but dead in the clouds. Her bosom almost bare, her legs draped in stockings the color of the Nazi's uniform, she lies inert in the heavens, her body almost impaled on the soldier's thrusting bayonet. To her right and immediately above his helmet, a white flower exfoliates strangely from the column of smoke or bed of clouds that has emerged from the traveling locomotive and drops a single white drop—tear, semen, or blood, it is impossible to say.

This cover drawing, integrating as it does elements of conventional Nazi symbolism in a surrealistic landscape of sexual desire and death, sets the tone for the *The White Hotel*, an intricately plotted novel that tells the story of Elizabeth Erdman. She is the daughter of a Russian-Jewish father and Polish-Catholic mother, and her pains, both physical and mental, constitute the primary focus of the narrative. The reader first gets to learn of Elizabeth, or Lisa, as she is more commonly called, through some passing references to her in the opening pages, which present an imaginary exchange of letters between Freud and some of his colleagues. In these letters Lisa is referred to as "a young woman suffering from a severe hysteria," whose writings show her to be the victim of "an extreme of libidinous phantasy combined with an extreme of morbidity." "It is," says Freud, "as if Venus looked in her mirror and saw the face of Medusa." Both faces are prominently portrayed in the novel, which itself is a complexly drawn portrait of the combat between Eros and Thanatos. As Lisa says at one point, "If I'm not thinking about sex, I'm thinking about death. Sometimes both at the same time." Hence Freud's judgment that his patient "was suffering from a severe sexual hysteria," a condition made graphic in her writings.

These writings, in verse and in prose, are the product of an imagination whose intense sexual preoccupations are everywhere shadowed by hallucinations of the most fearful kind. Lisa's sexual fantasies combine elements of pornography with images of cosmic disaster; not only does the feminine body yield itself endlessly to the pleasures and pains of erotic indulgence, but the sexual activity is accompanied by visions of spectacular ruin brought on by flood, fire, landslide, and fatal accident. Orgasm is everywhere attended by and seems almost to bring on a series of catastrophic deaths. Taken together these scenes of apocalyptic violence comprise what Thomas refers to as "the landscape of hysteria." It is both Lisa's mental landscape and, as the book's later chapters reveal, part of the characteristic landscape of twentieth-century history.

To Freud, who analyzes Lisa's writings in a case study called "Frau Anna G.," the poor woman is beset by "an inflated imagination that knew no bounds." Through the classic procedures of psychoanalytic investigation, Lisa's sexual problems are minutely dissected and traced back to homosexual tendencies deriving from childhood trauma. Her visual hallucinations, which accompany and interrupt her sexual play, are shown to be screen memories of early, repressed encounters with parental trespasses. And her physical ailments—she suffers from chronic pain in the left breast and pelvic region—are the punishments that the unconscious inflicts upon her as "the price of her freedom from intolerable knowledge." Freud's conclusions about Lisa's difficulties transcend the particular pattern of self-injuring behavior that belongs to the hysteric and begin to confirm his growing sense that the human condition itself involves "a universal struggle between the life instinct and the death instinct"; in this respect, Elizabeth's illness does not so much separate her from the rest of us as it exaggerates and highlights the eternal contention between the forces of life and death.

The representation of Elizabeth Erdman as a victim of severe sexual hysteria explainable in analytic terms takes up nearly half of *The White Hotel.* Much of the remaining half is devoted to upsetting Freudian theory through Elizabeth's belated confession that she has withheld vital information from her analyst and hence intentionally misled him. The effect is to expose the "mythic" or fictive basis of psychoanalysis and to seriously call into question its conclusions. The Freudian method is ingenious and, in its own terms, coherent, but as *The White Hotel* will thereafter take some pains to show, the truth of suffering is such as to transcend all attempts to explain it theoretically. The violence of history, and not psychic violence, is at the heart of the human condition.

To make poignant this line of historical thinking, Thomas redirects his novel in a way unanticipated by everything that precedes it in the course of its first 200 pages. For nothing about Lisa's story foreshadows her death at Babi Yar, the site of her final suffering. Nevertheless, although her sense of herself as a Jew is, at best, peripheral, her fate is to be that of Jewish fate at its most tragic, and her story ends in an extremity of pain that far surpasses that of hysterical ravagement.

Thomas's chapter on the Nazi destruction of the Jews at Babi Yar is the most powerful in the novel, but it raises a number of serious questions, the first of which has to do with the place of the Babi Yar material in the novel: Is it natural, and does it, in fact, "fit" the narrative? There seems to be nothing about Lisa's story earlier on that leads logically or inevitably to Babi Yar. There are several suggestions in the opening chapters that Lisa is clairvoyant, but previsions of the Holocaust are not a very credible part of this novel's progress, and the author's attempts to explain away Freudian explanations of her pains only to situate them suprarationally in the contexts of this century's most extreme instance of historical catastrophe are unconvincing. The Jewish tragedy is an awfully chastening reminder that human suffering transcends our ability to comprehend it, it is true, but to invoke tens of thousands dead at Babi Yar as the means to delegitimize Freudian theory is to burden this novel with a historical weight far in excess of what it can easily carry. As a result, the narrative is thrown out of proportion, forced as it suddenly is to accommodate a terror infinitely greater than the terrors of a single body or mind. When Lisa is trampled by a Nazi boot in the ravine of mass death, her chronically aching breast and pelvis, however one understands them previously, are suddenly to be seen as early warning signals that history is about to take a turn into human holocaust. If one result of this revelation is to move the narrative away from the rational control of Freudian explanation, another is to force the reader to endorse a vaguely defined occult mythology that embraces telepathy, something that most readers will have difficulty doing.

Another problem raised by this section of *The White Hotel* results from the author's use of A. Anatoli's [Kuznetsov's] *Babi Yar,* in which he found the story of Dina Pronicheva, a Jewish survivor of the massacre at the ravine. Thomas acknowledges his debt to this book on the copyright page of the novel, the customary way of putting to rest any questions of propriety that might arise; nevertheless, it is difficult to recall so total a reliance on a previous literary source as here. The Babi Yar chapter is so heavily derivative, in fact, as to call into question whether an author's normal acknowledgment is sufficient in this case. For Thomas has taken from Anatoli's *Babi Yar* not only many of the key names and episodes of his historical re-creation but in numerous instances has carried over into the prose of *The White Hotel* whole passages of description virtually verbatim.

That issue aside, just what is the place of this chapter in the larger scheme of the novel, and how does it clarify the character of Elizabeth Erdman as the reader has come to know it up to the point of the Babi Yar massacres? While the genesis of imaginative literature is always something of a mystery, it is clear in this instance that Thomas was powerfully moved by the story of Dina Pronicheva that he found in Anatoli's book and that he modeled his own Lisa largely on her. But to what end? Why has he seen fit to rely so heavily on the earlier author's account, to the point of carrying over whole sections of it into his own writing?

These questions can be answered not so much by recognizing the close and constant parallels between Lisa's fate and Dina's as by noting the one or two major differences in their stories, differences that help to distinguish history from fiction. Dina Pronicheva is said by Anatoli to be the only eyewitness survivor of Babi Yar; Lisa is made to be one of its innumerable victims. But apart from this crucial fact, what really distinguishes the actual survivor from the imaginary victim is that, in the moment before Lisa's death in the ravine, Thomas forces her to undergo a horribly cruel rape by a sadistic Ukrainian guard, who uses his bayonet to penetrate her, whereas there is no mention in Anatoli's account that Dina Pronicheva ever was violated in such a brutal and obscene way. In this case, Thomas has departed from his source and is freely inventing, in order, one imagines, to bring to a high point the morbid sexual fantasies of the earlier part of the novel:

> An SS man bent over an old woman lying on her side. . . . He drew his leg back and sent his jackboot crashing into her left breast. She moved position from the force of the blow, but uttered no sound. Still not satisfied, he swung his boot again and sent it cracking into her pelvis. Again the only sound was the clean snap of the bone. . . . He went off, picking his way among the corpses. . . .
>
> The woman, whose screams had not been able to force a way through her throat, went on screaming; and the screams turned to moans, and still no one heard her. In the stillness of the ravine a voice shouted from above: "Demidenko! Come on, start shoveling!"
>
> There was a clatter of spades and then heavy thuds as the earth and sand landed on the bodies, coming closer and closer to the old woman who still lived. Earth started to fall on her. The unbearable thing was to be buried alive. She cried with a terrible and powerful voice: "I'm alive. Shoot me, please!" It came out only as a choking whisper, but Demidenko heard it. He scraped some of the earth off her face. "Hey, Semashko!" he shouted. "This one's still alive!" . . . "Then give her a

fuck!" he chuckled. Demidenko grinned, and started unbuckling his belt. . . . [He] yanked the old woman into a flatter position . . . [and] yanked her legs apart.

After a while Semashko jeered at him, and Demidenko grumbled that it was too cold, and the old woman was too ugly. He adjusted his clothing and picked up his rifle. With Semashko's assistance he found the opening, and they joked together as he inserted the bayonet, carefully, almost delicately. The old woman was not making any sound though they could see she was still breathing. Still very gently, Demidenko imitated the thrusts of intercourse; and Semashko let out a guffaw, which echoed from the ravine walls, as the woman's body jerked back and relaxed, jerked and relaxed. But after those spasms there was no sign of a reaction. . . . Demidenko twisted the blade and thrust it in deep.

This fictive elaboration of Anatoli's text is a sickening but by no means singular instance of the literary imagination's perverse attraction to the Nazi atrocities, especially as these begin to take on a sexual character and feature the female victims of violent crime. As already indicated above, the sexual desirability of the mutilated woman is a recurring motif in fiction about the Jewish tragedy and is one of its most blatantly exploitative strains. One finds it in writers of high culture as well as in the more popular literature and always toward the same end: the evocation of new forms of erotic sensation through a concentration on sordid and atrocious experience. One imagines, therefore, that Thomas, like others before him, was drawn to the documentary literature of the Holocaust not so much for historical reasons but in order to mine it for fresh metaphors of sexual violence. It is noteworthy that what the novelist seems to find especially compelling in Anatoli's recounting of Dina Pronicheva's story, in fact, is what is left out of it, namely the details of her sexual ravishment, a ravishment that never took place. Since *The White Hotel* is concerned less with history than with myth, though, Dina's story is "completed," and the needs of an utterly cruel sexual mythology are served, through one final, vicious penetration of Lisa. Crushed by an SS boot and assaulted by Ukrainian bayonets, the Jewess goes to her agonizing death in a final paroxysm of passion, her body "jerking back and relaxing, jerking and relaxing." While Babi Yar was one of the great slaughter pits of World War II, it is invoked in this novel ultimately to provide a bloody bed for murderous orgasm with a Jewish woman who is already a corpse.

In surveying this fiction, one sees the pattern repeated time after time:

in the places where mass suffering once was, prurience has come to be. Out of *anus mundi* there has come "inspiration" in the form of fantasies of "power, politics, pornography, and mania." "Oh, what ghoulish opportunism are writers prone to!"

V

Domesticating Hitler

It's like old news now, Auschwitz.
The *new* news is . . . seeing Hitler
like a human being, at home,
treating a little kid nice,
making love to a woman.

—*To the Eagle's Nest*

WE LEARN, IN TIME, to accustom ourselves to all kinds of things, even the worst—even Hitler. For that to happen, though, the bad news has to be toned down some, shorn of its terribleness, tamed to suit temperaments not used to prolonging a sense of unprecedented misfortune. The trick is not to turn the bad news overnight into good news, but to translate it into terms that are manageable and thus to make a place for it that will seem natural. Fictions help in this process—indeed, they motivate it, chart its course, make it possible; otherwise, one would be altogether at the mercy of history, that burden of consciousness that Nietzsche opposed in a famous essay as a condition of eternal sleeplessness "that injures and finally destroys the living thing, be it a man or a people or a system of culture." Better, said Nietzsche, to cultivate the artistic sense and live with pious illusions.

Among our most favored pieties are those we attach to history itself to render it comprehensible, and hence a bit more tolerable. We like, for instance, to see connections between beginnings and endings and have cultivated some elaborate fictions to explain how people and events follow one another in patterns of meaningfulness that seem to be not only coherent but crucially determined. Nietzsche was not far off the mark when he called this sense of history "disguised theology," but we would do better to look to a more recent expositor of the phenomenon to explain it.

If fictional beginnings are calculated to engage a reader's attention, fictional endings are the surest test of a book's integrity and credibility. The story that fills the time between the two, as Frank Kermode argued persuasively in *The Sense of an Ending*, is more often than not a reflection of a comprehensive "fictive" sense of history and finds a paradigmatic base in long-persistent theological constructs. In bringing these to light, Kermode pointed in particular to apocalyptic types, or fictions of the End, which tie up the randomness and diversity of experience in neatly structured sequences of beginning, middle, and end. Our understanding of how we commence and how we conclude, he explained, is largely a function of "fictions of concord," which operate not only in the world of books but also in shaping our sense of the world at large.

So long as these fictions are retained *as* fictions, Kermode went on to argue, they may serve a useful purpose, but "if we treat them as something other than they are we are yielding to irrationalism; we are committing an error against which the intellectual history of our century should certainly have warned us. Its ideological expression is fascism; its practical consequence the Final Solution." Nevertheless, "the regress to myth" is a commonplace in modernist literature, and, as Kermode convincingly showed, it is not difficult to convict some of the major writers of the century "of dangerous lapses into mythical thinking" of an apocalyptic character. Accompanying the passion for imaginary endings, he warned, is a passion for universal bloodshed, only on the other side of which is there believed to be the possibility of renovation and redemption. Before the eschaton, though, there is the strong temptation to adjust one's sense of the world we inhabit to the regnant fictions, an adjustment that, Kermode concluded, "insults reality" by wrenching it into conformity with some very dangerous illusions, the most pernicious of which is antisemitism.

These are sobering thoughts and can be of direct consequence for a fuller understanding of some of the fictions under review here. Beyond that, Kermode's insights can help to illuminate the larger fictions that lie behind our fascination with Hitler and with the near-historical apocalypse he brought on. Finally, they can help to direct our thinking about fictions that transform Hitler's own end by denying or reshaping its historicity.

The White Hotel is a prominent case in point, for its visionary ending seems to confirm some of Kermode's suspicions about the entanglements of apocalyptic desires with fantasies about Jewish fate under the Nazis. Given the bloody and painfully prolonged slaughter scene at Babi Yar, the novel concludes on an odd and altogether unanticipated note of concord, a note that seems radically incongruous with the narrative line that precedes it. For instead of culminating the sufferings of Elizabeth Erdman in the ravine, where, once brought to that point, her story properly ends, Thomas transports her and many of the other dead to a place beyond death vaguely called "The Camp" and vaguely resembling Israel. He has, in other words, given his novel a decidedly religious, specifically Christian ending, invoking as he does several of the key New Testament place names and people (Emmaus, Cana, the Jordan River, the fishermen) and, in a final coda, invoking the Christian love ethic: "I think wherever there is love, of *any* kind, there is hope of salvation. . . . Wherever there is love in the heart." These words, supposedly spoken by a resurrected Elizabeth, seem little more than sentimentalism and can hardly overcome the tragedies that precede. Nothing in the previous chapters anticipates them or prepares the reader to accept "salvation" as the likely end-point of Lisa's fate. Yet she is made to utter pious words of hope in the book's final pages, including verses from The Song of Songs ("Many waters cannot quench love, neither can the floods drown it"), which she could hardly be imagined to know, let alone recite. Yet she is said to sing them—at one point even in Hebrew—just as, after her gruesome ordeal in the mass grave, she is referred to romantically and improbably as "the rose of Sharon." Moreover, Lisa learns that her mother, who perished in a hotel fire years before during an adulterous affair with her uncle, is really not dead at all but has just joined her in "The Camp": "The only important, terrible thing had been the *death;* and now she knew that didn't apply, for her mother had not died, she had emigrated."

The place to which she had "emigrated" is pictured as a paradise for all souls, an Israel of the spirit. In an ecumenical touch that calls to mind the popular advertisement for Levy's rye bread, Elizabeth comes to realize that "you did not have to be Jewish to be here," that her Polish-Catholic mother indeed "was on the lists." Given all of these miraculous occurrences (they even include a fatherless birth), one should not wonder that at novel's end Lisa's chronically ailing pelvis and breast cease hurting, and she runs off to take up the duties of a nurse and aid new immigrants arriving in this haven beyond the grave. As unbelievable as it may seem, the last word of *The White Hotel,* a novel memorable for its graphic depictions of blood and pain, is "happy."

What can one conclude about this odd and disconcerting conclusion? Not that D. M. Thomas is a poor writer, for he is not, but that at book's end he suffered either a loss of judgment or a loss of nerve and sought easy recourse in a myth of denial. "Myth" in this sense of it, though, is a much poorer, much less compelling thing than its heuristic counterpart at the opening of the novel, where it points to "a poetic, dramatic expression of a hidden truth." The largest hidden truth in *The White Hotel* is the one that links sex and death. While there is nothing in this novel that necessitates situating this linkage in Babi Yar, once the narrative does carry Lisa there, which is to say, once it begins to simulate history, there is no credible way of escaping the authority of actual events, especially events that trace back so recognizably to a source as prominent and powerful as Anatoli's *Babi Yar.* Yet escape Thomas does—at first through a mythology of erotic indulgence, then again through a mythology of spiritual transcendence of the weakest and most evasive kind. Neither way is capable of revealing the hidden truth that lies at the heart of this fiction or of disclosing anything of consequence about the dread history that underlies it. Fiction in this deflated version of it is little more than make-believe, a poor substitute for the more substantial mental and imaginative work necessary to bring the novel to a more fitting conclusion.

Anatoli ended his own book by stressing the moral responsibility for remembrance, a responsibility made urgent by the desires of those who would forget history or, still worse, deny it. "A former high-ranking officer in the Gestapo declared recently in an interview that there had never been any death camps, ovens, or gas-chambers, that all such things had been invented by propagandists. He stated, quite simply, that they had *never existed.*" In the years since Anatoli wrote these lines, the Gestapo officer has been joined by a great many others who would also like to undo the Holocaust by weakening the tenacity of memory that keeps it alive. "If you tell them out loud, to their faces, that they are being deceived," Anatoli went on, "they won't listen. They will say it is only a malicious slander. And if you produce facts, they just won't believe you. They will say: 'Such things never happened.'"

To be sure, Thomas's mode of Christian sublimation is not nearly so blatant a defamation of history as this; nor is it the primary responsibility of novelists to document or otherwise to reinforce the facts of history in their writings; but if they do bring themselves to invoke actual events, it becomes a matter of some importance that their work not contribute to the erosion of historical memory through even the remotest subversion of facticity. The death camps, the ovens, and the gas chambers did exist, and in the wake of their existence there are no immediate happy endings possible, in literature any more so than in life. Far from conjuring up easy restorations and reconciliations in some fictive paradise beyond, the truth of fiction in such cases must be as severe and unsparing as reality itself was at Babi Yar. Otherwise, there is the chance that Babi Yar and so many other places like it in the mass graveyard that was Nazi-occupied Europe will in time appear to be little more than macabre fictions themselves, from which the dead can gain their release by emigrating to a welcoming haven beyond. Such a "regress to myth," as Kermode calls it, makes for neither good theology nor good fiction and needs to be handled with a high degree of skepticism.

One should be equally skeptical about the ending of William Styron's novel, for it, too, strains after catharsis and recovery. At the conclusion of *Sophie's Choice*, Sophie is dead, Nathan is dead, six million Jews, two million Poles, one million Serbs, and five million Russians are dead (the numbers are Styron's), but Stingo, the author's narrator, is said to be healthy, awake, and ready to begin a new day. "Blessing my resurrection," he says, "I inscribed the words: '*Neath cold sand I dreamed of death/but woke at dawn to see/in glory, the bright, the morning star.*" And that is the end of the matter: Auschwitz as a bad dream, to be shaken off with the coming of a new day and the scribbling of some maudlin poetry.

While in most other respects *The White Hotel* and *Sophie's Choice* are very different kinds of books, they share a common desire to conclude their narratives of extreme personal and historical suffering on a visionary note of transcendence. One sees this same tendency as well in writings about the Nazi period that make no pretense to being fictive at all but still seem to require a fiction of concord or consolation to "overcome" the terrible history they brood upon. Consider, for instance, the writer Mary McCarthy commenting on Hannah Arendt's *Eichmann in Jerusalem:*

> To me, *Eichmann in Jerusalem*, despite all the horrors in it, was morally exhilarating. I freely confess that it gave me joy and I too heard a paean

in it—not a hate-paean to totalitarianism but a paean of transcendence, heavenly music, like that of the final chorus of *Figaro* or the *Messiah*. As in these choruses, a pardon or redemption of some sort was taking place. The reader "rose above" the terrible material of the trial or was borne aloft to survey it with his intelligence. No person was pardoned, but the whole experience was brought back, redeemed, as in the harrowing of hell.

At first glance, this is a highly original reading of *Eichmann in Jerusalem*, but in fact it is very much of a piece with *The White Hotel* and *Sophie's Choice* in its projection of a "happy" ending to an otherwise brutal story. Ms. McCarthy favored tropes of transcendence—those soaring, exhilarating, triumphant images of redemption—because, as she freely admitted, not to have them would be to confront a history that was simply overwhelming in its record of pain. Instead, she found in Arendt's book a "plot and lesson" that "were almost a godsend." In her own words, "the episodes that stood out were those that dealt with the Jews who were saved—the happy endings. They were the redeeming features of an otherwise unbearable history. . . ."

Since most Jews were in fact not saved, their story remains unbearable and is unrelieved by the narrative consolations of "plot and lesson." Void of redeeming features, it does not easily or naturally make up into a conventional fiction, least of all one with a "happy ending." Yet as one reads Thomas, Styron, and McCarthy, among others, it is evident that the need to strive against a hopeless history is strong and results time and again in fictions that have at their heart a myth of denial.

Such denial may take many forms, but its intent is always the same: to substitute an alternative mythology or fictitious history for events whose factual character one cannot abide. In the writings we have been looking at thus far in this chapter, the central tropes are all the result of a desire for transcendent truth, although, as has been argued, these "truths" very rarely ring true. Still, while the fictions are weak, the motivations behind them are not basically malevolent. The same cannot be said for certain other recent writings, whose aims are not to transcend but to traduce the terrors of history, and thus to eliminate them altogether from consciousness.

The most blatant example of this kind of willful substitution is to be found among the so-called revisionists, who have attempted to erase the

Holocaust from historical memory by outright denial of the Nazi program of genocide. To them, there simply was no such thing as the *Endlösung,* and all claims to the contrary are dismissed as a "hoax" invented to serve "Jewish interests." Thus, they have sought to disclaim the presence of gas chambers in the Nazi death camps or even to deny that such camps ever were established in the first place for the purpose of murdering Jews and others opposed to the Third Reich. The "hoax," which is entirely of their own making, is especially pernicious, for as it is developed through the pages of the revisionist journals, it assumes the guise of historical scholarship and seems to take on the character of authenticity. Authors with Ph.D.'s trailing behind their names, some of whom hold college and university teaching posts, regularly participate in a campaign of disinformation that mimics scholarly research but has as its sole purpose the undermining of the scholarly enterprise. For those who know the historical literature about the Third Reich, it is not difficult to expose the work of the revisionists for what it is—mostly bogus, malicious invention—but to the public at large, perhaps slightly in awe of academic-looking publications filled out with footnotes and "scientific" graphs, it is just possible that "revisionism" may begin to persuade.

As of this writing, the revisionists have no standing at all in the scholarly community and seem to be making only minor ripples in the consciousness of the public at large. Their desire to rewrite the history of World War II by denying its very worst features is not shared by most Americans, although here and there journalists on the lookout for deviant types are able to turn up an occasional social studies teacher or small-town preacher who may advocate the "revisionist line." What is of interest about revisionism, therefore, is not its impact, which is trivial, but its motivation and the fact that its exponents feel that times have changed enough to allow them to broadcast freely the most poisonous lies about Hitler's crimes against the Jews.

Once one recognizes these fabrications for what they are—cruelly conceived, if not self-evident, fictions—it is possible to see them as the furthest extension of trends within popular culture that have the effect, if not necessarily the aim, of diluting the historical sense by translating the most gruesome events of the recent past into pseudohistorical fantasies. The pornographic indulgences illustrated in the previous chapter are only one expression of a dalliance with the symbolism of the Nazi era for pleasure's sake. Another teases the mind not so much with the prospect of new erotic possibilities but with metahistorical ones. What, for instance, would have happened if Hitler had succeeded in snatching Churchill out of England and bringing him to Germany? That is the intriguing possibility raised by Jack Higgins's best-seller *The Eagle Has Landed*. ("At least fifty per-cent of it is documented historical fact. The reader must decide for himself how much of the rest is a matter of speculation, or fiction. . . .") Or, more drastically conceived still, what would have happened if Hitler had actually overrun England, executed Churchill by firing squad, burnt Buckingham Palace, and imprisoned the King of England in the Tower of London? These are the questions at the center of Len Deighton's best-selling *SS-GB*. In *To Catch a King*, also written by the author of *The Eagle Has Landed* (then under the name Jack Higgins, now as Harry Patterson), the quarry is the Duke of Windsor. In Stephen Marlowe's *The Valkyrie Encounter* the target is Hitler himself, his hunters a group of dissident Wehrmacht officers intent on saving Germany from the Nazi regime.

For all of their individual features, these are pretty predictable books, employing as they do the proven formulas of popular novels of espionage, suspense, and international intrigue. The common link among them is the leading conjecture "What would have happened if?" coupled with dramatic references, both historical and pseudohistorical, to Hitler's Reich. As recreational reading, they offer their supply of thrills in ways that do not seriously tamper with historical understanding, because no one who reads them is under the illusion that they aim to offer serious judgments on any part of the historical record. In all of these respects, the popular novels bear no resemblance to the work of the revisionists, which by its very nature sets out to corrupt the mind, not entertain it.

Whether one looks to distort historical understanding or distract from it, though, the effect of indulging the mind over the matter of Hitler's crimes is the same: one turns gross historical pain into something else, something far less appalling than it in fact was. In the first instance, the crimes of the Third Reich are diffused by lies; in the second, they disappear into light entertainment. In both cases, the real character of Hitler's Germany gets thinned out, for whether one tunes in for fun or is turned away by the deceptive manipulations of a bogus "scholarship," one begins to be a little less shocked by the historical truth, a little less conscious of its severity. In a short time, it becomes possible for the imagination to domesticate even Hitler himself.

It is not necessary to love him in order to set aside imaginative room for his return, only to see him as a little less menacing than he was, and hence a little more like all the rest of us. That is the secret behind virtually all of the fictions that project a Hitler who survived the fall of Berlin and is still alive somewhere today. In Pierre Boulle's "His Last Battle," for instance, Hitler is an old man living with Eva Braun in peaceful retirement in a Peruvian mountain village. It is 1965, twenty years after the close of the war. Hitler gardens, raises hogs and chickens, paints, lives a relaxed and leisurely life. He and Eva have adopted a boy of mixed blood, a half-caste, who is sent into town to meet a guest and accompany him home to the family compound. The guest is Martin Bormann, who finds his erstwhile Führer "younger and infinitely more alive than the figure of the human wreck who had left the bunker twenty years before." Of late, though, his health has been bad, and Eva worries about the condition of his heart. She tells Bormann not to bring up bad memories from the past, for they make him agitated and get him needlessly upset. And when he is upset, she reports, he loses sleep, perspires, and falls into a stammer. It all seems to have something to do with the Jews. In order to gain some peace of mind, Hitler has been talking with a local priest and now seems close to some point of resolve. He is seventy-six years old, not a good age to live with an overburdened conscience and unnecessary anxieties. The two decades that have passed since the end of the war have been good to Hitler. His mountain retreat has been calming, and his untroubled life there has allowed him to build "a new body" and "a new soul." Moreover, he has "changed on certain points" about the past and now wishes only to be able to die at peace with himself. But memories of the Jews assail him—"importunate, nauseating memories." At story's end, after prolonged and painful wrestling with his conscience, he declares to Bormann, who is himself haunted by guilt over the murder of six million Jews, that he has won through to victory:

> "The Jews, that's it. . . . But I've won. . . . And who could, who would want to, harbor resentment in a setting like this? It took me a long time to make my decision, but it is final. I have driven all hatred out of my heart. . . . The Jews, Bormann, the Jews—I have forgiven them."

The story turns on that final line, which one immediately sees is not the expected declaration of remorse and atonement but merely a piece of self-deceptive apology. The irony, a weak one, is intended to confirm the idea that, whereas in so many other ways Hitler may have changed, with respect to the Jews his thinking is still perverse. Other serenities of the soul aside, Hitler is still recognizable in his heart of hearts as Hitler.

Or is he? For whatever its other intentions may have been, "His Last Battle" develops an image of Hitler that, until its final line, largely de-demonizes him. Hitler as gentleman farmer, father, husband, recreational painter, and garden architect is hardly to be distinguished from any of the fifty thousand retirees living out their last years in Sun City, Arizona. The years he has spent in the serene setting of his mountain retreat cultivating exotic plants and flowers, raising bees, and caring for his little family have changed him in some fundamental ways and made him far more recognizably human. His antisemitism remains endemic, as the conclusion of the story shows, but if one can allow him his strangely tortured feelings about the Jews, everything else about the man shows him to be a model citizen—sensitive to the beauties of nature, skillful and responsible in the administration of his property, benevolent in his relations with the native villagers, an entirely respectable husbandman and neighbor. The Jews aside, he is, in his present incarnation, more or less like one of us.

In C. S. Forester's "The Wandering Gentile" he is a far more agitated figure. Nervous, driven, half-berserk, Hitler wanders the highways of America, hitching rides with Eva Braun, looking to reach Washington, D.C. to make a last-ditch political deal of some kind to save his power. In contrast to the settled, rural lord of the manor of Pierre Boulle's story, Forester pictures his Hitler as a new version of the Wandering Jew—forever homeless, restless, suffering the punishments of an eternal exile. There is nothing admirable about the man, nothing in the story that brings one to especially sympathize with him. Eva, however, is something else again, for in her self-sacrificial loyalty to her distraught and helpless husband she is the very model of faithful female companionship. She guides her Hitler through all his troubles, soothes him, tends his every need, and throughout their ordeal together is a wonderfully responsible and calming presence. While her husband may be a tattered, ill-tempered, loony old man, there must be something about him that warrants the retention and love of this admirable and utterly dedicated woman. Compared to the Wandering Jew, who in most versions of the archetype is pictured as solitary and companionless in his misery, the Wandering Gentile doesn't have it so bad.

In Richard Grayson's astonishing story "With Hitler in New York," he has it, in fact, pretty good. Grayson has given us a Hitler in blue jeans, who backpacks his way to New York on Laker Airlines to spend some time with his Jewish girlfriend. As the story opens, the narrator is waiting at Kennedy Airport with Ellen, Hitler's girl, for the flight to come in. Hitler arrives from Germany wearing a work shirt and leather jacket, and they go off to the city. It's summertime, and New York is in the grip of a heat wave. They watch T.V., eat ice cream, smoke a joint together. The narrator notes that "Hitler had a nice air about him" and admires the way he moves ("He is so comfortable with his body"). Hitler is jet-lagged and dozes off on the couch. "What do you think of Hitler?" Ellen asks. "I kind of like him," the narrator says. "I never realized he was so witty."

As the story progresses, these early good feelings about Hitler increase. "I think I would like to be like him," the narrator muses. And later, "I wonder if I am beginning to fall in love with him."

Hitler is uncomfortable in the oppressive heat of New York and is catching a cold, but he doesn't want to put a damper on things and rallies his spirits. They go off to have breakfast at McDonald's, watch a movie together on Channel 9, have dinner in the Village. It's a little bit like the threesome in *Jules and Jim*. They gather a fourth, Libby, and go to Washington Square and sit around the fountain. The next day they swim, have dinner at Ellen's parents' house (the narrator's mother "seems to like Hitler," even if Ellen's mother doesn't), walk the boards of Brighton Beach, and eat eggcreams. Nearby some Russian Jews are enjoying themselves singing Yiddish folksongs. Hitler listens intently, understands the slightly bawdy lyrics, then walks off before he can be recognized by the old Jews.

The friendship between Hitler and the narrator deepens as the days pass. As an expression of his affection, Hitler gives the narrator a present, a book of Rilke's poems.

The remainder of their days together in New York are spent in pretty much the same way. The three friends have dinner together at a Szechuan restaurant in Brooklyn heights, sample the carrot cake at a healthfood place on Atlantic Avenue, look at the brownstones, joke around.

In the midst of it all, the narrator's grandfather dies in Florida, but the narrator does not want to skip out on a going-away party for Hitler, who will be flying back to Germany in two days, and does not tell anyone about the death. He feels bad about it, but it's Saturday night, their time together is now very short, and he joins the other guests at the party.

Hitler is a big hit, holds his beer well, and is as friendly and as witty as can be. The narrator's admiration has by now turned to love, and it is clear that they have become the best of friends. They get drunk and joke about winning the Nobel Prize together, Hitler for Peace, the narrator for Literature. "We would have to wear ties," Hitler says. "No, tuxedos," the narrator replies. "And top hats and canes." They joke some more about doing vaudeville together.

At story's end, the narrator confides in his new friend that his grandfather has just died, and begins to cry. Hitler consoles him by telling him funny stories. It helps some, and the narrator drives Hitler home feeling a little better. And there the narrative ends.

Substitute almost anyone else for Hitler, and the story would fail. With Hitler in it, though, it is a fictional tour de force, the furthest extension to date of the neutralization of the historical Hitler and the normalization of a new image of the man. The evil monster is gone, as is the murderous antisemite. One neither fears nor loathes this Hitler, for in developing him Grayson has eliminated from his narrative virtually every trace of the Nazi Führer and put in his place a regular guy—likable, affectionate, funny, fun to be with. In costume, manner, taste, and overall affability he fits in; in fact, he is something of a swinger and the epitome of the late-60s casual style. If one identifies at all with the narrator (and the story is designed to bring about an alignment of the reader's feelings with the narrator's), by story's end one hates to see Hitler go.

It is not difficult to see what Grayson has done in writing his Hitler story, but at the same time it is not easy to know why he has done it or how he wants his readers to understand it. Unlike other fictions that manipulate the survival myth, Grayson has put "With Hitler in New York" under no obligation whatever to explain how Hitler survived the siege of Berlin and his own suicide and is still around today. The story, in fact, is free of all references to the war years, the Nazi regime, the persecution and murder of the Jews, bunkers and bombs. In all of these respects, the story is unanchored in the history of the Third Reich and without the taint of any of its crimes. If there is any suspicion that this Hitler is sadistic, it is only because he throws his girlfriend around in the swimming pool. Otherwise, there is nothing at all brutal or mean-spirited about the man. Were his name not Hitler, indeed, one would not even pause to inquire about the possibilities of a mean streak, for this fellow is a softy, not a sadist.

He is also not an antisemite, as his affectionate ways with his Jewish girlfriend show clearly enough. There are indications that the narrator is also a Jew, and yet Hitler and he become the best of buddies. It is true that Ellen's mother does not take to him, but he gets along well enough with her father and is invited to share a meal at the family table. Hitler's ways with the Jews, in sum, are by and large natural and easy and bear no resemblance to the mad antisemitic passions of the Führer of the Third Reich.

Grayson, one comes to understand, has de-Nazified Hitler, pacified him, and projected him as normative. At some very deep level of the imagination he has removed him from history, recast him in anti-apoca- lyptic terms, and made him safe to behold. His name and nationality aside, Hitler might as well be someone else, someone one need not fear to touch or tangle with romantically. There are no ironies here, weak or strong, only erasures so complete as to disarm the historical sense al- together and eliminate it as a factor in reading. In its representation of Hitler as a pure fiction, "With Hitler in New York" carries us beyond the transcendental leaps of the religious imagination, beyond the counterfeit claims of the revisionists, beyond the "alternative" possibilities and fictitious endings of popular formula fiction, and into a realm of imagina- tion that all but dissolves historical memory. Whatever its author's inten- tions may have been, his story succeeds in showing us just how much is lost when the name Hitler gives up its force and no longer evokes any- thing of consequence from the past.

"Forgetfulness," Nietzsche wrote, "is a property of all action. . . . One who wished to feel everything historically would be like a man forcing himself to refrain from sleep, or a beast who had to live by chewing a continual cud." The fictions reviewed in this chapter are a diverse lot, but all have in common a will to forgetfulness, the desire or ambition to spit out the historical cud. One does not read them and retain very much of the past, this despite the fact that all are premised upon a specific moment from recent history. Because the narrative thrust in every case is either unhistorical, antihistorical, or superhistorical, the past is soon left behind, dissolved or superceded by fictions that project endings other than those that belong to events themselves.

It should be clear by now that the literary afterlife of events often bears little resemblance to what in fact may have occurred in the world outside of books. "Art has the opposite effect to history," Nietzsche knew, and usually stands over against it in an adversary relationship. The implications of this opposition for our understanding of representation at large are profound and to this day have not been adequately understood. With respect to the particular problem of representation being pursued here, though, understanding should be a good deal clearer.

To put the matter all too simply and matter-of-factly: as writers take him up and transfer him onto the page, the historical Hitler changes shape and begins to evolve as a fiction. This is the case whether an author specifically intends it or not, for it belongs to writing *as* writing to transmute as well as to transmit images and events from the past. Images from a history as extreme as that of the Third Reich are especially prone to a variable existence, for they are surrounded by feelings of the most turbulent sort and are not easily mastered. Indeed, it is not unusual for them to do the mastering and to determine the shapes they will assume. That is the point of Ray Bradbury's "Darling Adolf," a story about the shooting of a film about Hitler and the confusions of identity that beset everyone involved in it. As the actor playing Hitler goes deeper into his role, it becomes unclear to what extent he is acting and to what degree he is being acted upon by the powerful and not always controllable image he has assumed. Playing the leading Nazi, filming him at Nuremberg, and being Nazi are almost one and the same, and, at least for a time, it emerges that to imagine the man is to become him. A similar point is made in Joseph DiMona's *To the Eagle's Nest*, in which, against the will of the producer, the director, and the actors, an anti-Hitler film (*The Secret Life of Hitler*) "was becoming a *pro*-Hitler film, despite the screenplay." In this case, as in the previous one, attributes of the demonic are said to overleap the limits of time and space and find an unintended revivification in art.

If one could confine the afterlife of images to art, the question of representation would be pretty much an aesthetic one, but, as is well known, it is hardly possible to predict the course of a powerful symbol once it is made manifest. The posthumous career of Hitler shows in more than literary ways how a fascination with strong historical types time and again overleaps the formal controls imposed by art and, as Kermode explained, follows illusion into the world, where it is likely to do more than a little mischief. The Nazi myth, which has been pursued in these chapters in its development through fiction, never has been content to settle for a merely narrative existence, and while it may have "plot and lesson" behind it, "story" is not its ultimate ambition. Power is, in the sense of some deeply perverse and predictably destructive desire for power-grabbing and power-wielding. But before power can be seized and violently released, the images of power have to be cultivated and made accessible, very much in the ways we have been noting. Thereafter, there is nothing except some pious hopes about good sense and moral scruple to keep the evil dreams of power-crazed mythomaniacs confined to stories. If one lives with a Hitler-obsession, after all, why not give it its full due and follow the hero's own course beyond art and into the world of homicidal fantasy?

One thinks, in this connection, of certain bizarre cases in public life where imitations of Hitler, or something close to them, transcended the boundaries of literary representation and took on the look of the real thing. Just what was Gordon Liddy up to, for instance, when he concocted his deadly *Nacht und Nebel* scheme to "silence" those he believed to be opposed to President Nixon's re-election plans? Here, from the recently published autobiography, *Will*, is an account in Liddy's own words of his plans for a covert intelligence and terror operation:

> DIAMOND was our counterdemonstration plan. At the time, we still expected the [Republican] convention to be held in San Diego. . . . I proposed . . . to identify protest leaders, kidnap them, drug them and hold them in Mexico until after the convention was over, then release them unharmed. . . . The sudden disappearances, which I labeled on the chart in the original German, *Nacht und Nebel* ("Night and Fog"), would strike fear into the hearts of the leftist guerrillas [as would] a team slated to carry out the plan as a "Special Action Group." When John Mitchell asked "What's that?" I knew . . . that Mitchell, a Naval officer in World War II, would get the message if I translated the English "Special Action Group" into German. . . . It was a gross exaggeration, but it made my point. "An *Einsatzgruppe, General*," I said, inadvertently using a hard g

for the word *General* and turning it, too, into German. "These men include professional killers who have accounted between them for twenty-two dead so far, including two hanged from a beam in a garage."

Liddy's *Nacht und Nebel* scheme is the kind of thing one would expect to find lifted out of a spy thriller or cut from some popular film on the Nazi period. The fact that it was neither but a real-life scenario that appeared only a decade ago in the upper reaches of American political power is chilling, for it shows in the most shocking way that the Nazi imagination operates well beyond the confines of frivolous and exploitative books and is afoot in the world. To see it at its most vivid, one needs to look well below the level of pulp literature and grade "B" movies at forms of the demotic that are all around us but nevertheless not easy to grasp.

How, for instance, is one to understand the likes of Frank Spisak, who in 1982 shot and killed three people at Cleveland State University on the grounds that he had a mandate to "liberate people from Jewish control and keep blacks from overpopulating and ruling the world"? When apprehended, Spisak was wearing a White People's party T-shirt emblazoned with a swastika. In court, he appeared in Hitler mustache, short-cropped hair cut over one eye, and brown military-type suit. He carried with him a copy of *Mein Kampf,* regularly gave the Nazi salute, and strongly objected to being tried as a criminal. "I am a prisoner of war in the war being fought between the forces of darkness and the forces of lightness," he declared, and went on to identify "the forces of darkness" as being "Satan and Satan's children, the Jews." He had a "mission," he told, to kill the blacks and the Jews, especially "black men" and "Jewish lawyers." The *Cleveland Plain Dealer,* which reported at length on the Spisak case, noted that the F.B.I. uncovered a "treasure trove of Nazi memorabilia" as part of Spisak's possessions. Nevertheless, it could print a headline that asked, in half-inch letters, "Spisak: Real Nazi or Fake?"

The headline questions whether Spisak should be judged legally sane or mad, but from the standpoint of this study, it hardly matters one way or the other. If sane, then the Hitler role was consciously and deliberately chosen; if insane, then the particular forms that madness takes are highly relevant to understanding imaginative possession and the specific cultural codes that are appropriated by an unbalanced mind. In either case, Nazi is as Nazi does, and the adoption of the Hitler persona in order to mimic Hitlerian behavior is but one more confirmation of the currency and potency of images of the Third Reich, images that for years now have been generously broadcast by the popular media and that will not necessarily remain confined within the controlled fantasies of art. In Spisak's case, as in Liddy's, to look at only two recent examples from the upper and lower reaches of American popular culture, it is clear that precious few distinctions between "fake" and "real" Nazi were observed; rather, something strongly compelling in the Nazi type overleapt its imaginative source and sought expression in the world at large. Power, especially the perverse use of power, is obviously not a matter to be confined to the page.

And yet it is not to be understood as altogether free of the page either, for, in its inception, power—that is, as Hitler saw it, the unrestrained, nihilistic use of force—begins as an idea on the page and takes on an extraliterary life only when and as conditions allow for a regress to myth. Hitler, as everyone knows, was a writer before he was a political leader of any consequence, and declared himself in prose well before he ever formulated policy for his nation. His words preceded his deeds by years, during which time he learned to conjure his fantasies into powerful forms of public oratory and political action. At the end of his life, as his final "political testament" indicates, he was still not finished with the words, which he used, right up to the very end, in the form of invective and assault. In this instance, as in so many others throughout the terrifying years of his rule, he saw himself as an artist in action. His "art form," if one can call it that, was the curse, which he brought to a kind of volatile perfection and propelled forward in ways that were unstoppable during much of his lifetime and that seem to linger on still today, four decades after his death.

To round out this lengthy metacritical excursus on post-Hitlerian indulgences and imprecations and to demonstrate to what degree we still live under the sign of Hitler's curse, it may be instructive for the reader to learn of a recent incident that brings into focus the links between the literary and extraliterary possibilities pursued by the Nazi imagination. As always, there was first a text, in this case in the form of a typed letter sent anonymously to the only synagogue in the small midwestern town where the author of this book sits and does his writing. The letter warned in ominous terms that "he" will soon be returning and that "they," Hitler's faithful followers, are already here and watchful. Moreover, it promised the local Jews that they would be hearing again soon from "him." And it signed off with a thunderous "Heil Hitler."

A crank letter. A bit of belated Nazi bravado. The stale rhetoric of an outworn, discredited creed. Empty threats from an empty mind.

Three weeks later, even as chapters of this attempt to study latter-day imaginings of Hitler were in progress, the synagogue was burning.

VI

Hitler, Jews, and Justice

> " 'I appeal to your sense of justice,
> your notorious sense of justice.' "
>
> —HITLER to the Jews, in *The
> Portage to San Cristóbal of A.H.*

> Hitler ought to live on as a Jew.
> —ELIAS CANETTI

JUSTICE, ONE OF THE noblest and most necessary of our dreams, insists that the punishment be appropriate to the crime. What, then, would be proper retribution for a synagogue-burner? Here are some prospects to ponder: the criminal would have to rebuild the sanctuary he destroyed, brick by brick, reciting the whole while the biblical Book of Lamentations; he would replace the Torah scroll he burnt by learning the ancient art of the scribe and copying out in faultless Hebrew calligraphy the full text of the Five Books of Moses; he would personally apologize to each and every member of the congregation whose prayer life he disrupted by reciting the penitent's prayers for forgiveness—annually, on the anniversary of his crime; he would labor to understand the essential wrongness of his deed by carrying out the most serious study of the arch-criminal who inspired him to arson in the first place—Adolf Hitler (but *not* by reading most of the books under review here, which would only incite him to escalate the level of his aggressive fantasies).

Justice, in this ideal conception of it, does not in the first place seek to take away so many years of the criminal's freedom or so much of his fortune but to force him to reflect upon his transgression and to rectify it by acts of corrective behavior. Because it aims to straighten, balance, realign, justice is not primarily punitive in nature but redemptive, and has as its goal the rebuilding and not the wasting of a human life.

Or so one would like to believe. In the real world, though, things do not necessarily happen that way: either the criminal goes uncaught, or he is apprehended and put away, sometimes for longer, sometimes for shorter periods of time, after which he may take up his can of gasoline and a match and look to repeat his hateful crime. Nevertheless, the dream of justice remains a possible one, even an indispensable one, and, among our culture's reigning fictions, it is among the last we would ever want to give up.

Usually, we like to think that justice has a universal application and, when administered by wise and impartial judges, works to assure the protection of each of us equally before the law. That being the case, one can understand readily enough how those who willfully break the law are subject to just punishments. What punishment, though, would be appropriate for Adolf Hitler? Had he lived, would it have been possible to conjure just retribution for him?

No, for one confronts here not just a series of infractions of the law but lawlessness itself, not a man whose errant ways brought him to crime but the essence of criminality. Penal solutions, it is obvious, would be less than meagre, for to sentence Hitler to the lowest circles of Dante's hell would be to assign him too easy a fate. As for educative or corrective measures, the man seems so absolutely overtaken by evil as to be beyond the reach of human redemption. Unable to devise proportionate forms of punishment, the imagination of justice comes up short in the case of Hitler.

In a legal sense, the failure is a hypothetical, and hence a harmless, one, for inasmuch as Hitler put a bullet in his head, the vexed question of justice drops away. As a problem for representation, though, it still remains very much alive, for precisely how Hitler is retained in memory and imagination is a matter that bears fundamentally on our sense of historical equity. With respect to what we are given to see and, through the accuracies or errancies of sight, to understand and evaluate, therefore, one can speak of just and unjust images—configurations of mind that are more or less truthful, erroneous, serious, capricious, sincere. The outcome of the contestation among these varied images is no small matter, for as they compete for our imaginative attention and allegiances, they begin to affect the ground of apperception itself. Images, no less than codified laws, are bound up with and influence our sense of proportion, balance, the nature of what belongs; they guide and define vision, affect moral valuation, help to determine the weight and substance of memory. In all of these respects, we are to no small degree at the mercy of the makers of images, and a frivolous or malicious distortion of certain powerful figures, just as a willful subversion of certain foundational laws, contributes in time to confound some fundamental sense of who and what we are as historical beings. For all of these reasons, one is indebted to judiciously drawn images just as one is to judiciously administered laws, and on pretty much the same account: they keep back the sundry confusions of chaos, anarchy, madness, and terror.

With respect to Hitler, there has been a poverty and a tyranny of images right from the start. On the popular level, where hyperbole was intended to direct both perception and sentiment, the Führer was exalted as a new Nordic god sent to Germany to lead the country to prosperity and power. The elaborately staged public rallies, the visual blowups of Nazi poster art and propaganda films, the quasi-religious political sermons all projected Hitler as a figure of grandly ceremonious and more than heroic proportions, a new German messiah.

There were, of course, those who were not taken in by these swollen images. Brecht, for instance, preferred to see the Nazi leader in plainer terms and referred to him in his poetry as *der Anstreicher* ("the house-painter"). Hitler's aggressive side is glimpsed in Shaw's *Geneva*, a minor play of 1938 which developed a "Mr. Battler," the pugnacity of the man indicated but also undercut by the touch of conventional stage comedy. Auden sought an image to explain the compelling hold Hitler had over the millions and, in a famous poem, projected him as "a psychopathic god," a phrase later adopted by one of Hitler's biographers. Among the least compromised of his countrymen, Thomas Mann seems not to have known precisely how to understand so vexing and contradictory a figure, at times dismissing him as "our political medicine man" but also acknowledging him as a "genius," albeit genius in a phase of gross decadence and distortion. Mann also denounced him as a "pitiable idler" and "fifth-rank visionary," a "sly sadist and plotter of revenge," but was moved to claim him as "an artist, a brother."

In most Jewish writings, both during the period of the war and after, one typically finds no similar sense of fascination or fraternization. In fact, one finds almost no significant allusions to him at all. In Emmanuel Ringelblum's *Notes from the Warsaw Ghetto* Hitler is called "Horowitz," an unexpected and uproariously bizarre appelation but one of a piece with other comic code names in the journal and explainable as part of the vengeance that Jewish wit exacts upon its enemies. Elsewhere one finds intermittent references to "the Beast" or to some latter-day Haman, but not much else. Leslie Epstein, in a recent novel *(King of the Jews)* that is something of a fictionalized cartoon, alludes weakly to "the Big Man" in Berlin, and Alain Spiraux, in *Time Out*, another try at popular burlesque, uses a diminuitive form of his name ("Hitlerino") to refer, rather incredibly, to the child protagonist of his novel. Otherwise, reference fades into still more oblique and abbreviated forms, as in the bare use of initials in Ernst Weiss's *The Eyewitness*, or, more typically, into silence, as if the very pronunciation of his name was a curse that would bring on untold calamities.

The sum of these occasional allusions, abstractions, and surprisingly minor references is a paradox of a startling kind, although one that until now seems to have gone generally unnoticed: the people who, more than any other, suffered the most under Hitler have had the least to say about him directly. Jewish writers have written endlessly about the European catastrophe but have been strangely reticent about the man who brought it on. None of the major biographies of Hitler, for instance, has been written by a Jew. One is also hard put to find any significant poems, plays, or novels from the war years in which Hitler figures in a central way. While Jewish writers have chronicled the Nazi Holocaust in voluminous detail, producing more books than one can easily read in a lifetime, the principal perpetrator of the war against the Jews is for the most part missing from the corpus of serious Holocaust literature.

At least among the European writers—those closest to the sources of the Nazi destruction itself—the very name of Hitler has seemed to carry an evil potency and is not to be casually invoked. When it is mentioned, as in the ghetto jokes recorded by Ringelblum and Chaim Kaplan, it is always in a vein of aggressive wit or within the context of a curse. Otherwise, Hitler's name has been regarded by Jews in much the same way as Haman's name, as a stain upon language that is to be vigorously blotted out. In the case of Haman, the effacement is done at the Purim festival through a ritual enactment of uproar, the repeated waves of noise solicited by the public reading of the Scroll of Esther washing over the slightest mention of Haman's name in an effort to drown it out. No such ritual has yet been developed for the effacement of Hitler's name, which is still too recent a rent in the Jewish psyche and has not yet been exorcized by any similar act of the popular will. Rather, it is almost as if the name remains under a powerful taboo and is referred to, if at all, most often in oblique and indirect ways or, as seems to be the preferred case, is simply rendered inaudible by a consensus of silence.

If this analysis is correct, then we may be able to understand a little better the general absence of Hitler from a body of literature that he more than anyone else has brought into being. His shadow and weight are everywhere to be detected in the writings of the Holocaust, but his presence, for reasons given above, hardly at all. As for his name, even Brecht and Mann, two of his most strong-willed antagonists, could not easily bring themselves to pronounce it, the former representing him in weak dramatic guise as Arturo Ui, the latter relegating him to the borders of society as a slick charlatan and magician.

Seen against this background of general literary proscription, George Steiner's *The Portage to San Cristóbal of A. H.* astonishes. The astonishment does not lie in the fact of Steiner's authorship, for this is not the first work of fiction by Steiner nor is it his first treating the war years. The three stories collected in *Anno Domini* (1964) all rehearse moments of personal crisis brought on by the infinitely larger crisis of the Hitler period. The latter, however, is intentionally backgrounded in the fiction of *Anno Domini* and consequently is felt less as overt subject than as informing context. In the essays of *Language and Silence* (1967) a far more explicit attention is given to the Holocaust, especially as seen from the standpoint of language and the erosions it has sustained in the aftermath of a time when words were made the servant of political barbarism. From at least the point of this important collection of essays, then, Steiner's work has been drawn to reflections on the ontological status of language, more specifically to linguistic devaluation and dehumanization, the compelling focus as well for much of the writing in *Extraterritorial* (1971) and *In Bluebeard's Castle* (1971). Steiner's study of *Martin Heidegger* (1979) likewise devotes itself to probing the connections between historical descent and a kind of moral and linguistic obliquity, in this case as represented by one of the foremost philosophers of language whose life and work were both troublingly implicated in Nazism. The implication strikes to the heart of Steiner's subject, and there is no reason to imagine he could move away from it in his fiction any more than in his analytic and essayistic work. The latter, in fact, might usefully be seen as preparation for the novel, itself an elaborate rehearsal of the resourcefulness and hellishness of human speech.

One of the striking features of *The Portage to San Cristóbal of A. H.* is its immense feeling of physicality, a tangible quality of experience embodied in the dense jungle landscape that makes up the principal setting of the novel, but also, and even more dramatically, in the book's unusually varied landscape of speech. Both are vividly rendered, the first as a Conradian "green hell," the second as an extension of Steiner's long-term attempts to get at human motivation and conduct from the inside of language, through a fine probing, as it were, of the signals transmitted by syntax, inflection, and innuendo. The territory of swampland and jungle is densely, even brilliantly registered, but the boldest penetration in this fiction is into another kind of territory, that belonging to the dark underside of words and to those whose handling and mishandling of them may be as true a measure of character as any we possess.

In the realm of words and word power, one of the century's great wielders and corrupters of language, of course, was Adolf Hitler, the "A. H." of Steiner's title. It is difficult to think of Hitler, in fact, and not imagine the man *speaking*, an image reinforced by miles of film footage displaying him wielding his considerable histrionic skills over the mesmerized German citizenry massed somewhere below him. It is just this kind of image that introduces Hitler into the novel: "They say your voice could burn cities. They say that when you spoke. Leaves turning to ash and men weeping. They say that women, just to hear your voice, that women would tear their clothes off, just to hear your voice." As the narrative develops, Hitler's voice will remain a faint and enfeebled one until the very ending of the novel; in fact, through sixteen of the book's seventeen chapters Hitler says hardly a word and has almost no distinctive presence in his own right. Nevertheless, although we hardly see or hear him, he is the focal point of all significant attention and directs the words and actions of every other character involved with him.

In plotting the novel and filling it with a multinational array of characters, Steiner has sought to probe the nature of this involvement from half a dozen different points of view. His concern, in fact, is, until the very end of the narrative, less with Hitler than with the unsettling place he has assumed in consciousness, a place that Steiner aims to clear via a Conradian descent into the heart of darkness.

The journey is undertaken by a team of Israeli agents who are intent on tracking Hitler to his hiding place deep in the Amazonian jungles. For this search to take place at all, of course, Steiner has had to build into his fiction a version of the survival myth, one that claims, as the convention has it, that the German Führer did not die by suicide but escaped his bunker at the last moment and successfully managed a flight out of Berlin to a prearranged haven in South America. The story is hardly original, but it gives the author a narrative means to keep Hitler alive, not only in memory but in the flesh, and hence to make possible, and ultimately to force, an encounter with him. Imagine, so this novel asks of us, "What would you do if Adolf Hitler walked into the room?" Never mind that the man would now be past ninety, that his Reich crumbled into ruin almost four decades ago, that later dictators have also shown us the face of mass murder—if Hitler appeared before you, what would you do? Such a confrontation, so the novel insists, must take place, and while it would be unnerving, no other encounter would be more decisive, more revealing, more necessary. For Hitler was not just one murderer among many, one tyrant among other tyrants, but, in Steiner's view, the pivotal figure on whom the history of our time seems to turn, and hence the one above all with whom we have to come to grips.

But how is one to grapple with Hitler? Who among his victims and survivors stands ready to contend with him and to judge him? And what precisely would be the purpose of engaging him in trial? To put these questions in the language of the novel itself, "Exactly what is it he did to man?" and, after more than thirty-five years, "Who cares?" Who, even, wants to remember?

The novel raises these questions through a shifting point of view that brings into focus a many-sided interest in the person, career, and meaning of Hitler. Through a complex but neatly controlled progression of plot, the Israelis, British, Russians, Germans, French, and Americans all tune in to the Israeli tracking team, catching and interpreting the signals transmitted by their radio from the heart of the Brazilian jungles. After some hesitancy, a decoding of the messages brings the startling news: Hitler has been found by the Israeli trackers, who will attempt to bring him out alive. To British Intelligence, represented by Sir Evelyn Ryder, a character whose scholarly passions recall Trevor-Roper, this information is received with the keenest interest, the nature of which is chiefly forensic. To the Russians, still intimidated by earlier Stalinist practices, the capture of Hitler is a challenge to a previous era of politically motivated doctoring of the evidence about Hitler's last days, and especially about his suicide. The Germans are represented as taking an intense although abstract legal interest in the matter; the French want nothing so much as to prevent events from reviving too close an inquiry into the crimes of the Vichy government; and the Americans manifest both a blatantly commercial and diplomatically opportunistic interest in the affair.

None of these shorthand descriptions does justice to the novel's multiple point of view, which not only brings into focus the national preoccupations of the various interested parties but does so in the peculiar syntax and with the distinctive feeling of Israeli, British, Russian, German, French, and American sensibilities. Steiner's gifts as a polymath generally serve him well in these instances, and while there are moments where the portrayal of national characteristics begins to slide into caricature, for the most part the novel's international dimension is credible and bears out the notion that, with respect to Hitler, "No one wants him like anyone else. Each in his own little way."

As indicated above, Steiner has worked Hitler into his novel in such a way as to have him mirror back something deep in the national psyches of all who confront him. As such, he is a test of the strength and integrity of national will, of the truthfulness or evasiveness of individual stances toward history. Within these terms, the ultimate confrontation in the novel—ultimate for being most intimate, most intense, most obsessive—is, as it must be, with the Israelis. They, as representatives of the people Hitler wanted most, are the ones who most want him and who will see to it that they get him.

What keeps them on his track? In searching out Hitler, what precisely are they in quest of? The brilliance of Steiner's novel is that these questions are raised in such a way as to bring to a climactic moment of clarification a large part of the Jewish obsession with the Holocaust. This is achieved through a character whom we never see but whose voice directs the Israeli trackers to their quarry, drives them deeper and deeper into the dead air and fever-ridden swamps of the South American wastelands, scourges them with the most punishing claims of historical memory, and, by so doing, sustains them in their search. The voice belongs to Emmanuel Lieber,

> Emmanuel Lieber, whose fingers they were, often fumbling and ten thousand miles from arm's length, but his as surely as if he were now standing with them, dreaming the web, spinning and tightening it over the grid of the jungle, directing their racked, unbelieving bodies to the quarry, as he had for thirty years from London, then from Turin (where they had first, in worlds past it seemed, picked up the scent) and now from the small, unmarked office in Lavra Street in Tel Aviv. They were his creatures, the animate embers of his calm, just madness. Of a will so single, so inviolate to any other claim of life, that its thread went through Lieber's sleep producing one incessant dream. That of this capture.

If it is Lieber who drives on the Israeli hunters, it is the Holocaust that drives on Lieber. "The fires at Bialka, the children hung alive, the bird droppings glistening on the shorn heads of the dying," all this and more remains unforgettable to him, as it does to the Jews at large.

Following the Nazi immolation of European Jewry there are, in the words of one of the Israelis, only "two kinds of Jews left, the dead and those who are a bit crazy." Lieber is of the latter kind, a Jewish survivor of Hitler "who crawled out from under the burnt flesh in the death pits" and ever since has lived with a perception of life "so outside the focus of man's customary vision" as to mark him out as having "a piercing strangeness." If such strange vision constitutes craziness, then Lieber is indeed crazy, but no more so than Bellow's Artur Sammler or Schwarz-Bart's Ernie Levy or the Elie Wiesel and Pimo Levi of *Night* and *Survival in Auschwitz*. The "craziness" in every one of these cases is owing to a heightened not a distorted vision, a chastened form of historical consciousness that knows from experience "exactly what it is that Hitler did to man." In this respect, all Jews are a bit crazy and Lieber, as a representative Jew, is only one among many.

Still, he is the one singled out by Steiner to represent Jewish consciousness at its most acute, which in the post-Holocaust period means a consciousness possessed by historical memory at its most lacerating. To bear

the burden of such memory is to carry a weight of experience almost too
heavy for words to express, and as a result Holocaust literature is often
caught at a point of impasse between the imperatives of testimony and the
infirmities of language. Confronted by so intractable a dilemma, writing
frequently tends either to heighten into expostulation and apostrophe,
raising the voice to sometimes uncontrolled levels of utterance, or to drift
toward silence, extinguishing the voice in a dwindling sob of elegiac
lament. One of Steiner's extraordinary achievements in *The Portage* is
that he has found for Emmanuel Lieber a style that mediates between
these two extremes, a precise register of exclamation and lamentation that
simultaneously records and mourns, coldly enumerates yet carries an
immense affect.

André Schwarz-Bart achieved something similar in the memorable
ending of *The Last of the Just,* as Paul Celan also did in the compelling
rhythms of his famous "Todesfuge," but otherwise in the entire corpus of
Holocaust literature one would be hard put to identify a passage of poetry
or prose that surpasses the strength of Lieber's speech in the sixth chapter
of this novel. Like Schwarz-Bart's intermingling of the words of the *Sh'ma*
with the names of Nazi concentration camps, Lieber's discourse takes the
form and carries the tones of sacred litany; it lists and counts, lists and
counts, lifting name and number to the level of eloquence and consequence. Like Celan's stuttering and hallucinatory lyricism, it also drives
language into and beyond ellipsis, finding in fragments of speech a literary form to encompass and express brokenness. Prose of this order is rare,
and rarely sustained, yet Lieber's voice goes on and on, filling the pages
of this chapter with a kind of preachment that stuns the mind with its
punishing directness and clarity.

At the heart of Lieber's speech is history, chronicled rather than imagined, hypostatized rather than transformed. It is important to note these
emphases, for Jewish consciousness, at least that strain of it that comes to
expression here, is involved not in the making of myths but in the creation of conscience. For that task one does not look to the more emblem-
atical tropes of figuration but to the more disciplined resources of docu-
mentation. If, then, the Jews "are the people of the word," as one of the
characters of the novel declaims, it is the word stripped of its magical
potencies and dedicated to recording and vivifying factuality. Lieber's
"craziness," one comes to understand, is a function of his literalness: he

will not let go of the severe knowledge that experience has brought him or attempt in any way to turn it into symbolic meaning. It can have no such meaning, for it is beyond the transfiguring reach of metaphor and the modes of fictive imagining. For altogether different reasons, Hitler himself could not easily imagine it:

> Read what he said to his familiars, what he spoke in his dancing hours. He never alludes to the barracks or the gas, to the lime-pits or the whipping blocks. Never, as if the will to murder and the knowledge were so deep inside him that he had no more need to point to them. Our ruin was the air he moved in.

The description here is of a psyche that knows no distance between the wish and the deed, which in this case means between the imagination of murder and the bloody act itself. Hitler's mind as imagined by Lieber is one so infused by the passions of anti-Jewish obsessions as to leave no space for any sense of the Jew other than as deadly antagonist. In this respect, it, too, is a representative mind, exceptional only because it was endowed with the power to "make real the old dream of murder. Everyman's itch to clear his throat of us. Because we have lasted too long. Because we foisted Christ on them." Hitler, in this view of him, made a difference not so much because he espoused a new or different course of action toward the Jews but because his own kind of eloquence unlocked the passions that turned an age-old dream into day: "His words made the venom spill."

Although Lieber and Hitler never come face to face in the novel, the ultimate confrontation in *The Portage* is, as it must be, between them. Since Steiner keeps them physically apart, their encounter is represented as taking place on the level of language, or within language between two distinctly different attitudes toward the word, the one dedicated to representing the truths of history and the Lord of history, the other an apocalyptic assault against historical and theological thinking and the people who carry it forward into the world. This is not meant to suggest that Steiner reduces Hitler's war against the Jews to a language war, for that would be a trivialization and a distortion. However, inasmuch as Steiner looks to language as an establishing source of being and not only as its reflection, he is given to understanding radical semantic oppositions as being of the gravest historical consequence. If, as already noted, the Jews are the people of the word, they are so in a way very different from the way that Hitler was a master of words, a "word-spinner, mountebank":

> As it is written in the learned Nathaniel of Mainz: there shall come upon the earth in the time of night a man surpassing eloquent. All that is God's, hallowed be his name, must have its counterpart, its backside of evil and negation. So it is with the Word, with the gift of speech that is the glory of man and distinguishes him everlastingly from the silence or animal noises of creation. When He made the Word, God made possible also its contrary. Silence is not the contrary of the Word but its guardian. No, He created on the nightside of language a speech for hell. Whose words mean hatred and vomit of life. Few men can learn that speech or speak it for long. It burns their mouths. It draws them into death. But there shall come a man whose mouth shall be as a furnace and whose tongue as a sword laying waste. He will know the grammar of hell and teach it to others. He will know the sounds of madness and loathing and make them seem music. Where God said, let there be, he will unsay.

The biblical voice here is Lieber's, describing the voice of one dedicated to negating the Bible and "banishing God from creation." In this view, the nihilism of Nazism is understood as being in a perverse way theological and Hitler a kind of counter-Messiah or reverse-Jew. Within the terms of some derangement of mind, he is even imagined as being "the last Jew," one who has come to shut down history, or at least Jewish history, to throw off "the blackmail of transcendence," which he claims Judaism has pressed on the world, and hence return it to a pagan earthiness freed of any of the claims of conscience and the aspirations of the ideal.

These views come into the novel, and bring it to a climax, in Hitler's speech at the end of *The Portage.* Like Lieber's speech, this one also takes up a full chapter. The only significant utterance of Hitler in the book, it is spoken at an improvised trial before his Israeli captors and is meant to be taken, at least implicitly, as a reply to Lieber. It is, in fact, Hitler's self-defense, or at least the self-defense of a character in the book who is called by Hitler's name and charged with his crimes.

Before looking at this speech, some things need to be said about the kind of book Steiner's novel is and about certain generic qualities it shares with other fictions alluded to earlier in this study. It also seems necessary to speculate, if only briefly, on the connections between popular culture and high culture and on the interchange of images and values that takes place between the two. For what one sees in reading *The Portage to San Cristóbal of A.H.* against certain popular strains of imagining Hitler goes far toward rendering Steiner's A.H. a more understandable, and a vastly more troubling, figure.

In its main lines, *The Portage* is a thriller not unlike Ira Levin's *The Boys from Brazil* or Herbert Lieberman's *The Climate of Hell.* All three books are set in South America, all involve Jews in search of fugitive Nazis, all invoke themes of vengeance and justice. It may be only coincidental, but the name of Steiner's chief Nazi-hunter, Lieber, closely resembles that of the principal sleuth in *The Boys from Brazil*, Liebermann, which happens in turn to be the name of the author of *The Climate of Hell.* Whether a matter of happenstance or not, the family resemblance among all three novels is symbolized by more than this commonality of names: all three exemplify the thriller's fascination with criminality and its preference for developing sensational plots around dramatic and suspense-filled quests for figures of incarnate evil. A dalliance with horror, danger, and the prospect of further menace still to come is part of the peculiar pleasure the genre conveys. In teasing the mind with nightmare visions of imminent doom, the thriller looks to shock, but it also will typically balance the feelings of extreme fear it generates with the emergence of virtuous characters who counter, overcome, and defeat the sources of evil in the narrative. There are exceptions to this pattern, to be sure, novels that keep the reader's feelings of fright and apprehension keyed up even at the close of a book, but most thrillers are more merciful than this and resolve the tension of the plot by having the antagonist murdered or otherwise dispatched by book's end.

Steiner works within the main lines of these conventions but with a crucial difference: far from doing in his evil character, he allows him to prevail. What is more, he does so with a flourish, awarding to Hitler not only the privilege of making the longest single speech in the novel but the book's climactic one at that, in essence upsetting the genre's normal pattern of resolving the dramatic conflict in favor of the protagonist and projecting the villain as the more powerful, indeed the triumphant, presence in the book.

This reversal is made possible through Steiner's adaptation of a second popular genre—the trial novel. Such narratives typically have a strong ideological or political side to them and always turn on an author's skillful use of opposing styles of discourse to make their points. Characteristically employing dialogue in the form of disembodied oratory, developed often at great length and with all of the subtle skills of the rhetorician, trial narratives exist to present the clash of ideas. While generally uninterested in the complexities of plot development and the establishment of fully fleshed-out characters, they delight in the intricacies of argument and debate and appeal to readers who take a special pleasure in witnessing the vindication of a particular point of view solely as a result of the triumph of one mode of oratory over another. Consequently, such books can be cleverly specious, easily lending themselves to the linguistic schemes of sophists and casuists and, if not guided by a disciplined moral vision, can end up seeming to resolve complex historical and philosophical questions through the mastery of bewitching language games.

Given the exceptional investment that Hitler himself placed in the powers of language, it comes as no surprise to learn that he has been brought to trial time and again in popular fiction, but never before with the effect he assumes in Steiner's novel. In both Max Radin's *The Day of Reckoning* (1943) and Michael Young's *The Trial of Adolf Hitler* (1944), for instance, Hitler is easily vanquished by prosecutors who present charges against him that he is unable either to evade or to refute. Both novels were written and published during the years of World War II and undoubtedly were intended to show that the crimes of the Third Reich were as indefensible as they were brutal. One is hardly surprised to see, therefore, that in the end Hitler is sent to his death, which is precisely the outcome that readers on the Allied side would have expected. In a novel variation of the capital sentence pronounced in these two novels, Fred Allhoff's *Lightning in the Night* (1979), which was also originally published serially during the war years, has a humiliated and vanquished Hitler committing suicide on the ballroom floor of the Netherland Plaza Hotel in Cincinnati. In all three cases, it simply would have been out of the question for Hitler to survive, let alone prevail.

Closer to our own time, and appearing only a year before the initial publication of Steiner's novel in the *Kenyon Review* (Spring 1979), Philippe van Rjndt also summoned the German Führer to trial in *The Trial of Adolf Hitler* (1978), but with a difference: his Hitler is accuser as well as the accused and, in an impassioned if unconvincing defense before the judges of a world tribunal, he sets forth the view that he is no more guilty of war crimes than the British, the Russians, the Americans, and others. As for Nazi atrocities against the Jews, van Rjndt's Hitler argues, in terms that will be amplified by Steiner's Hitler, that the Jews courted animosity by their strange vocation as a people apart and that when hatred against them turned violent, virtually no one in Europe or elsewhere came to their defense. Thus, Hitler claims he acted not only "as the voice of the German conscience" but as the instrument of Western will in general. Otherwise, as he argues, "If Jews were such a precious commodity, why didn't anyone take them from me? I did not want Jews in Germany; the German people didn't want them. But when I placed nine hundred of them on a ship and it set sail, which country opened its arms to them? Not one!" Although he is able to win a debater's point here and there, Hitler fails to convince his judges that he was not guilty, his neo-Nazi supporters likewise fail in their attempts to educate a new generation of followers to establish a Fourth Reich, and at novel's end Hitler is taken away and shot—as the convention today would have it, by an Israeli paratrooper.

Hitler's bravado performance before the world tribunal at the United Nations, though, seems to indicate that the climate of feeling about the relative guilt of Nazi Germany has changed sufficiently for more recent fiction to accommodate a sustained and spirited, even if losing, defense of Adolf Hitler. Nothing of the sort would have been thinkable at the time when Radin, Young, Allhoff, and others wrote their fictions, every one of which presents a resounding indictment of Hitler and Hitlerism. By the time of van Rjndt's *Trial of Adolf Hitler,* however, sensibility had obviously altered, at least in its Western liberal strain, and it now became possible to see Hitler as no longer the only political criminal of the modern age. As this line of thinking likes to state it, if there was Auschwitz, wasn't there also Hiroshima, Dresden, Vietnam, and, as a late but telling addition, Beirut? Or, as the question is sometimes unsubtly put, does not the "spirit of Hitler" live on among those who suffered most under the Nazis yet today manifest "Nazi behavior" and commit "genocides" of their own?

In Europe, recent literature of the kind we are examining has extended this grotesque line of thinking in some especially macabre ways. In 1973, a vulgar and altogether perverse pseudohistorical novel was published pseudonymously in Germany by one "Sissini" under the title *Samuel Hitler*. In it, Hitler is fictionalized as a Jew. The idea of imagining the Führer in these terms is to show, in the author's words, that "history is not a one-way street" and that it is entirely conceivable that a German-Jewish statesman could have led his country on an aggressive course of nationalist expansion—even to the point of using atomic weapons to realize his goals. After all, so the author argues, was there not the precedent of England under the imperialist policies of the Jew Disraeli?

A year later, in 1974, Hennecke Kardel, a latter-day apologist for German National Socialism, brought out in Geneva a book entitled *Adolf Hitler—Begründer Israels* ("Adolf Hitler—Founder of the State of Israel"), in which a "half-Jewish" Hitler is recognized as the true architect of the modern Jewish state. Hess, Göring, Goebbels, Rosenberg, Frank, Himmler, Heydrich, and others are also mentioned as being somehow Jewish and in league with Hitler in doing Zionist work. Indeed, the volume ends with references to Ben Gurion and the establishment of the Jewish state, which, the author argues, would never have come into its own without the "help" of the Nazis. Not Herzl but Hitler, therefore, is the originator of the idea of the Jewish nation reborn in its ancient homeland.

These notions have been given wide currency recently in international circles. Add to them the Hitler films, the Hitler jokes, the innumerable television shows on the Third Reich, the serializations of countless stories about Hitler and the Nazis in newspapers and magazines, the revisionist histories by Irving, Butz, and others, and one begins to understand what motivated the *Frankfurter Allgemeine Zeitung* to ask if Hitler was emerging as "the Hero of the Seventies."

The "heroism" here referred to has nothing to do with valor, courage, or any other quality of spirit that one would deem admirable, but is attributable solely to the uncanny stature that Hitler now enjoys. Far from fading with the passing of the decades since his defeat and death, he has moved ever closer to the center of consciousness and is today a figure of inescapable presence. If anything, his image has intensified in recent years rather than diminished and, within both popular culture and advanced intellectual circles, has undergone significant transformation and even a degree of rehabilitation. While far from being either generally loved or admired, there is no doubt that he is closer to the nerve of current feeling, readily available for imaginative appropriation, and altogether more accessible as a figure within fantasy life than one might have suspected he would be some years back.

In trying to understand this phenomenon, one recognizes that it hangs together with a heightened interest in the Jews, the obsessive focus of Hitler's most ferocious passions, and especially with the Nazi war against the Jews, which itself is in the process of being popularized in forms that often make it seem only a cut above light entertainment. As already indicated, the most contemporary and most authentic writings of the Holocaust are notably silent about Hitler, but within popular categories he looms very large indeed. He does so as well increasingly within those circles that we like to refer to as belonging to "enlightened opinion." In fact, as the carriers of high culture absorb what is going on below them—and it is a truism about culture that those in the lower strata influence those above them at least as readily and rapidly as the other way around—it is inevitable that Hitler should become a figure of general preoccupying concern. Precisely *which* Hitler is emerging and will predominate is still an open question, but there no longer can be any doubt that a new mythology of the man and his times is in the process of developing and that various versions of it are today in contention with one another, in intellectual circles as well as among the populace at large. Given the unavoidable "Jewish question" that is always and everywhere linked to the question of the Nazis, it is inevitable that whichever imaginative projection of Hitler comes to prevail will be bound up with and strongly determined by particular attitudes toward the Jews. Indeed, there can be no imaginative apprehension of Hitler today without a concurrent imagining of the Jew.

All of this is a far cry from the silence surrounding the image of Hitler referred to earlier. One thinks in this respect of Karl Kraus, the Viennese Jewish writer, whose first remark on "the matter of Hitler" was that he had nothing at all to say—"es fällt mir nichts ein." The situation has so far reversed itself that not only do writers today not hesitate to say whatever they would like about Hitler but they invent things for him to say that he never uttered and probably could not have imagined. In other words, they make him up as they go along to suit whatever vision they have and would like others to have of Hitler and his infamous *Judenfrage*.

The lengthy speech that ends *The Portage* exemplifies this phenomenon in a most dramatic and most disturbing way. It is, in fact, the most sustained imagining of Hitler by a serious writer to emerge in recent fiction and brings to a point of culmination a number of the tendencies described in the preceding pages. On the level of rhetoric, the speech is in its own way a grand performance, but it is fraught with so many problems of historical error and moral dubiety that one's final response to the book as a whole is greatly complicated.

Even before the onset of the speech, one is confronted by allusions to Hitler that are bound to startle, if not to repel, most readers. Steiner's appropriation of the popular motif of the Nazi-Jew doppelgänger, for instance, conflates Lieber and Hitler so completely as to make the one a shadow of the other. In his word-drunk fanaticism, as in his obsessive and implacable drive for vengeance, the Israeli is said to be the absolute complement of the Nazi, without whom he would lead a life devoid of purpose. More plainly put, "They need each other like the breath of life," so much so that "to be a Jew is to keep Hitler alive."

Both live on as mouths—as *Spielers,* word-spinners, mountebanks. While Lieber's speech in chapter six is immensely powerful, it is superceded by Hitler's speech in chapter seventeen, which nowhere replies directly to Lieber's charges but seeks to overcome them through a combination of self-vindicating apology, contrived theological and historial argument, and self-serving, aggressively asserted counter-charges. Hitler begins, for instance, by claiming he invented nothing but took over his principal doctrines from the Jews, as these were taught to him by one Jacob Grill—"son of a rabbi, from Poland"—with whom he lived in a flophouse for male vagrants. Now, it is well known that as a young man Hitler actually did live for some three years in a *Männerheim,* or doss house, in Vienna, but if he ever encountered such a figure there as Grill, none of Hitler's major biographers has discovered him. One might think, therefore, that Steiner has made him up, which would be his privilege as a novelist but not much to his credit as a novelist of ideas working his way through some exceptionally weighty problems and with such a well-documented historical figure as Hitler as his mouthpiece. Actually, the problem of Grill is far more vexed than mere invention would suggest, for prior to Steiner's references to him, there is one place where he does appear, although it is a source that an intellectual of Steiner's seriousness and stature would not ordinarily consult—namely, Kardel.

Among the innumerable Hitler books currently on the market, Kardel's *Adolf Hitler—Begründer Israels* is surely one of the most bizarre and irresponsible; its historical value is nil, and its moral vision altogether corrupt; it is, in fact, a piece of blatant antisemitica. One is not surprised to find anything at all in such a book, therefore, including allusions to an eccentric sidekick and tutor to the youthful Hitler named Grill. Kardel portrays him as an ex-Catholic priest (and former Jew) who was wont to take long walks with Hitler through the streets of Vienna, during which time he initiated the future Führer into the mysteries of Jewish religious learning. Where Kardel found him is unclear, for, to repeat, no such Grill appears in any of the standard Hitler biographies. He occupies several pages in *Adolf Hitler—Bergründer Israels*, though, and reappears in the final chapter of *The Portage to San Cristóbal of A.II.*, where it is asserted that Hitler not only looked to Jewish teachings for the ideological under-pinnings of Nazism but actually had a Jewish teacher who indoctrinated him in Jewish concepts and beliefs. Because it is doubtful that such a person ever existed, the argument falls apart on historical grounds. Yet even if a historian one day turns up evidence that the young Hitler had known a Jew such as Grill who told him cranky stories about the Bible, the argument that Nazism originates in Judaism—a commonplace by now of antisemitic thought—would still seem meretricious.

The rest of Hitler's self-defense is similarly contrived, although it is spoken with such bravado as to make it appear to be a confident, strongly reasoned statement of fact. As one listens to it, though, and inevitably juxtaposes Steiner's Hitler with his historical prototype, it becomes clear that most of the terms of the argument and, even more so, of the particu-lar style of rhetoric in which they are presented point away from this fictitious Hitler and toward his creator as the true source of their perverse energy and brilliance. For try as one may to suspend disbelief and to allow a writer to fully indulge all the liberties of fiction, it is altogether unlikely that Adolf Hitler, the Führer of the Third Reich, would think or speak in the terms of this discourse, whose subtleties, ironies, and manifold histor-ical and theological allusions pass beyond the range of Hitler's mind. This judgment is made, to be sure, through references that are external to the novel itself, but the name Hitler is not a literary fabrication and, at least at this point in history, cannot be reduced solely to the fictive. Steiner manages to avoid this troublesome problem of representation until the end of his book by having people speak *about* Hitler but by having Hitler himself remain virtually silent. Ultimately, though, he must give him a voice, and one does not hear in it much that could have come from the mouth of the real A. H.

What one does hear, astonishingly, is a language that is recognizably Steiner's own, taken as it is from key sections of *In Bluebeard's Castle* and some of the author's other expository writings. The ideas set forth by the Hitler of *The Portage*—ideas that link Nazi doctrines of covenantal election, racial purity, historic destiny, and the like with biblical sources—have been presented by Steiner before in some of his nonfiction work. Now there is nothing wrong with returning to such work and mining it for a later novel, but to carry over not only the thinking but the distinctive idiom of one's earlier writing and ascribe it to Hitler is something else again, and something close to mimetic compulsion of the most desperate kind. Steiner has argued speculatively in the past that Nazism was a travesty of Judaism, that the Jews as the embodiment of conscience became intolerable to a Christian Europe that remained pagan at heart, that by introducing God, Jesus, and Marx into the world the Jews pressed upon a reluctant mankind a "blackmail of transcendence" that it could not abide and finally threw over in the explosion that was the Holocaust.

In making these formulations, Steiner challenged earlier arguments of both historical positivists and psychohistorians in an effort to get at what he believed to be some of the deeper cultural and religious strains of Nazism. There are those who have criticized this aspect of the author's work as being too conjectural and others who have found it unusually bold and perceptive. What baffles in this instance, though, are not Steiner's ideas but their transference almost verbatim into the mouth of Hitler, as if Steiner's understanding of Hitler were identical with the latter's self-understanding. Moreover, by releasing a number of his previously considered ideas into the mouth of Hitler, Steiner has reduced his thought from the more disciplined tones of exposition to the level of a pompous political harangue. A necessary distance between the author and his principal character has collapsed here, with the result that the novel ends on a note that is brutal, improbable, and jarring.

Why end it at all, in fact, with Hitler's speech? Why give Hitler the last word, one that sets forth not only to explain Nazism as a runaway Judaism but to vindicate the genocide of the Jews as the necessary historical spur to the establishment of the State of Israel? As the voice of Hitler is made to say, "Would Palestine have become Israel . . . had it not been for the Holocaust?" To frame a complex historical question in this way is to solicit a simpleminded answer, after which one is tempted to assent as well to Hitler's occult musing that follows: "Perhaps I *am* the Messiah," he declares, "the true Messiah, the new Sabbatai whose infamous deeds were allowed by God in order to bring His people home." According to this warped view of things, Hitler was as much the Jews' redeemer as their destroyer, a violent successor to Herzl who "made of the long, vacuous daydream of Zion a reality." As he himself arrogantly suggests to his Israeli captors, to whom he pleads for a generous award of justice, should they now "not be a comfort to my old age?"

Whatever one's understanding of Zionism and Israel, the reality that looms largest here is neither religious nor political but rhetorical. Steiner's Hitler is involved in the devil's game of language subversion, a game that his historical prototype brought to a kind of deadly perfection. The deadliness lies in appropriating a vocabulary of sacred terminology and inverting it so that words are evacuated of their customary meaning and made to take on a reverse signification. It is this process that characterizes the grammar of hell and makes the sounds of madness seem like music. To close the novel on this note is to succumb, rhetorically, to the seductive eloquence of negation, a closure that appeals to the very same instincts courted with such devastating effect by Hitler himself. While one is no longer surprised to see such a grotesque development in the writings of the revisionists, one winces to hear the ghost of Hitler cackle triumphantly in a novel by George Steiner.

The novel was published in this country on April 30, 1981, the anniversary of Hitler's suicide. It has since been adapted for the stage by Christopher Hampton and has played in both England and the United States. The reviews have been mixed, with most tending to be highly critical and some unambiguously damning. In every case, it is the Hitler speech that the reviewers fix on, for it is this speech that brings the drama to its high point of theatrical and, by implication, political expression. The reviewer for the *New York Times* condemned the play outright, charging that its "principal effect is that of distortion, the use of theater to dull political awareness." The reviewer for the London *Times Literary Supplement* was only slightly less harsh, criticizing the Hitler speech as a "harangue" that mixes "bad rhetoric, special pleading, and misapplied logic" and concluding that "you cannot deal with the Holocaust in these terms without turning it into hollow artifice . . . which breaks apart with the first breath of reality." Others have written similarly about the play, some dismissing it as a "travesty" and "obscene."

Critics will be critics, and there doubtless will be some who will write more favorably. Among the reviews that have appeared, the most telling by far is the one carried in *The Observer*, for it provides a look into the audience's response to the play as well as the reviewer's. Commenting on the long Hitler speech, delivered with exceptional affect for a full twenty-five minutes by the gifted actor Alec McCowen, the reviewer notes that at play's end, "instead of a horrified silence, there was an immediate storm of applause and shouts of 'Bravo.' I think these were in some measure for Hitler as much as for McCowen. Steiner had brought Adolf Hitler back to life and crowned him again."

If this reading of the audience's reception of the play is at all close to being correct, then Hitler's appeal for a "justice" that will vindicate him, while denied by his Israeli captors, has been more than minimally met. Lieber's speech, for all of its power, has long since been left behind, and, in the play as well as in the novel, it is Hitler who compels the most intense interest and who will remain as the most permanent legacy of Steiner's efforts. First "the Hero of the Seventies" and now a popular favorite of London's Mermaid Theatre: could Hitler possibly have envisioned a more successful posthumous career?

And could Steiner have envisioned such disastrous effects? As a scholar who has devoted sustained attention to the "subtle, corrupting fascination" of the Nazi crimes, he could have. And as a critic who has taken others to task for searching the hideousness of the Holocaust for literary inspiration, he should have. What, then, accounts for his developing such an intense image of Hitler—a Hitler of eloquent, if malignant, grandeur—as the A.H. of *The Portage?*

The answer, I suspect, has something to do with the psychodynamics of polemical fiction, or at least with the nature of the author's engagement with such fiction. Steiner, as is well known, is an accomplished, even elegant essayist. But the art of the essay is characteristically one of reflection, discrimination, and evaluation, not of representation. The essayist makes distinctions, delineates, judges, but rarely attempts to show or to embody. Explanation is the essayist's art; incarnation, the novelist's.

In imagining his A.H., Steiner, it is clear, set aside the disciplines of mind associated with essayistic composition and allowed himself to be flooded with novelistic possibility. In his own words: "The book was written at a single go in 1975 and 1976 in Geneva. . . . With many of my other books I would say I wrote them; with this one I would simply say it wrote me." While there are creative advantages to this kind of composition, there are also dangers, paramount among them the danger of imaginative possession by other minds. One can, after all, be seduced as well as inspired by the zeal of fictional invention, ravished as well as imaginatively replenished by the energies of myth. Both tendencies are evident in the novel, which shows its author seized by as well as seizing upon his central character.

Steiner was strongly taken by the histrionic Hitler, in whom he believed he had discovered a family resemblance to "the people of the word." Since he has long defined the Jewish vocation as essentially linguistic, and since he likewise understands the power of Hitler as rooted in the power of words, the temptation to incarnate the Nazi Führer as an exaggerated type of the Jew must have been strong. As essayist, Steiner probably would have resisted it, but as fiction writer he felt free to follow it out and ended up projecting a Hitler who not only wantonly defies the historical record but does so with a bravado that appeals to the worst of human passions. Moreover, in an awesome lapse of judgment he gave to Hitler the authority of his own essayistic voice, but pitched now to express an exuberant mockery of his Jewish adversaries—indeed, a mockery of every major aspect of Jewish antecedence. In what is clearly calculated to be a triumph of rhetorical disputation, Hitler exonerates Nazism by establishing it almost as a movement within Judaism and then vindicates himself by blaming his Jewish victims for the crimes he committed against them. As for those who survived him and reestablished the Jewish nation in Israel, they are in his view little more than the by-products of his own inspiration, and capable of being every bit as cruel.

The appeal of Steiner's Hitler, in short, is the appeal of cleverly formulated Nazi apologetics in combination with stridently stated antisemitic invective, a potent combination in Hitler's day and, if George

Steiner's novel is any indication, still available for imaginative appropriation and revivification today. Whether there is a public that will be receptive to this rhetoric and open to the passions it can provoke remains an open question, but if the applause at the Mermaid Theatre is in any way representative of a more general mood, the curtain may be about to go up for many more reruns of the hero of the Third Reich in posthumous triumph.

VII

Pop Culture, Politics, and the Iniquity of Images

The key to modern myths is in the
banality (taken seriously) of kitsch
success and the popularity of
triviality—final traces of worlds gone
under. Hitler and his people were
the best performers of those
things. . . .

—HANS-JÜRGEN SYBERBERG

The opposite of history is not myth.
The opposite of history is
forgetfulness.

—ELIE WIESEL

THE LONG-LEGGED, high-kicking beauties in Mel Brooks's *The Producers* look like any other chorus line of dancers but for a single exception: they are suited out in the black uniforms of the SS. The dance they perform, backed by a second chorus line of Valkyries, is called "Springtime for Hitler" and is meant to be a musical burlesque of Nazi antics. The number mixes mock-politics with female flesh, high-spirited farce with showy extravaganza. It finds a parallel in Brooks's most recent film, *To Be or Not to Be*, in a bizarre song-and-dance routine called "Naughty Nazis." In both cases, one looks on and laughs.

A skit on the popular television show "Saturday Night Live" portrays Hitler and Eva Braun fumbling over one another like two clumsy teenagers in heat. It's silly and stupid but probably just funny enough to get a laugh. Not so *The National Lampoon* Hitler jokes, which are neither naughty nor funny but mostly just vulgar, tasteless, sick. Nevertheless, they continue to appear, so someone must like them. Is it the same crowd that listens to the popular singer David Bowie croon about "visions of swastikas in my head," that snaps up the premier number of Larry Flynt's new magazine *The Rebel* because it features a huge swastika on its cover, that likes wearing punk styles that use Nazi symbols as fashionable emblems of a new social defiance?

One could multiply these examples many times over, but that would only belabor the obvious: the signs and symbols of the Third Reich have become part of the common language of popular culture and are today all around us. In England, according to the Alternative Holiday Catalogue, one can even "vacation" in a Nazi-style camp, "complete with barbed wire, searchlights, watch towers, and fifty guards in SS uniforms." This idea of an Auschwitz-as-theme park has not yet crossed over to this side of the Atlantic, but there is still plenty of opportunity for those who want to fantasize about the "naughty Nazis." You can giggle over the Nazi buffoons of popular television shows, flaunt the swastika as your personal badge of disaffection, ogle the girls in the high black boots. For the children, there is *When Hitler Stole Pink Rabbit* and such "simulation games" as "Gestapo: A Learning Experience about the Holocaust."

In sum, Hitler has become a gag, an adornment, a piece of the fun. If one cannot yet talk about the arrival of a Nazi chic, one can say that it is easy—and in no way regarded as a sign of gross social deviance—to indulge a taste for the stylistic gestures of a latter-day pop fascism, although a fascism commonly regarded as being without political implications. As the owner of a London boutique for punk fashions explains, "They like the Nazi things because they are interesting decorations." Is it possible that it never crossed the lady's mind that "the Nazi things" have a history of some consequence behind them?

It is possible. A prolonged dalliance with Nazi-inspired fun-and-games—with countless jokes, fads, films, fictionalizations: the whole run of popular and pornographic indulgences—not only dulls political awareness but dissipates and ultimately defeats the historical sense. Laugh at Hitler often enough, dress him up as a stage villain, convert him into a cartoon of frightful or ridiculous demeanor, and in time you will no longer know who or what he was. Play with the symbols of his Reich as if they were harmless toys and before long the distractions of mind generated by the pleasures of lighthearted amusement weaken the sanctions of historical memory. "Holocaust" then comes to mind more readily as a popular television show than as an unprecedented crime within history. As for Hitler, rendered commonplace, he becomes a conventional focus of the leisure and entertainment industries, even something of a pop hero. According to David Bowie, Hitler was "one of the first rock stars." To catch him in a musical setting, you can, if you wish, listen to some of the songs of "Pink Floyd" or tune in to the English rock opera *Der Führer* and hear Eva Braun sing, in a voice of moony enchantment, "When I'm leaning against his shoulder, the bad times are over."

With such goings-on as these, the bad times may be only just beginning. While probably none of what has been described above is specifically intended as "pro-Nazi," its inevitable effect is to undermine any sane vision of culture and ultimately to erase the fingerprints of Hitler from a history of mass murder. To popularize the man and his crimes is to trivialize them and, in time, to render them almost invisible. Here, in the words of Saul Friedländer, is one prominent example of that process:

> A few months ago I saw Joachim Fest's film, *Hitler: A Career*, in a movie theater in Munich. The dazzling rise, the titanic energy, the Luciferian fall: it is all there. As for the extermination of the Jews, a few words in passing, no more. An inconsequential shadow of this grandiose tableau. For anyone who does not know the facts, the power and the glory still remain, followed by a veritable vengeance of the gods. . . .
>
> For anyone who does not know the facts, the mystical communion with the brownshirt revolution and its martyrs still remains.
>
> Thus is evidence transformed over the years, thus do memories crumble away.

The role of art in the erosion, as well as the establishment, of historical memory is fundamental, for most people do not have a primary relationship to "the facts" and learn about them secondhand, through the mediations of word and image. With few exceptions, we "see" what we are given to see, "know" what we are given to know, and thus come to retain in memory what impresses itself on us as vision and knowledge. We owe to the Czech writer Milan Kundera the insight that such knowledge has the deepest political consequences, indeed that "the struggle of man against power is the struggle of memory against forgetting." One can, in this sense, talk about art's implication in a politics of remembrance as well as a politics of forgetting, an implication not lost on any writer who sifts through the debris of history in an effort to reconstruct the past or on any national leader who is alert to the legendary or mythic dimensions of the past and has the gift of reviving them for his own political objectives. In both cases, the refashioning of the past need not be determined by any special fidelity to history, as if the latter has been fixed once and for all and is no longer malleable to the pressures of mind or imagination; rather, the appeal to the past follows the course of feeling—of dream, impulse, hope, or wish—and makes of the "facts" new fictions of desire.

What happens to our sense of reality as a consequence of these developments is obvious to any reader of contemporary fiction or any observer of contemporary politics. As the novelist E. L. Doctorow put it a while back, "There is no longer any such thing as fiction or non-fiction; there's only narrative." In the words of the same author: "What's real and what isn't—I used to know, but I've forgotten." William Styron carries this line of thinking beyond Doctorow's playful agnosticism to his own more deeply felt historical relativism:

> Facts *per se* are preposterous. They are like the fuzz that collects in the top of dirty closets. They don't really mean anything. . . . A novelist dealing with history has to be able to say that such and such a fact is totally irrelevant, and to Hell with the person who insists that it has any real, utmost relevance. . . . Certain facts . . . can be dispensed with out of hand, because to yield to them would be to yield or to compromise the novelist's own aesthetic honesty. . . . A brute, an idiotic preoccupation with crude fact is death to a novel, and death to the novelist.

Styron's desires as a novelist—or the imperatives of what he calls his "own aesthetic honesty"—brought him, in writing *Sophie's Choice,* to refashion Hans Frank, the Nazi Governor General of a large part of occupied Poland, as a Jew, and to make Rufolf Höss, the Commandant of Auschwitz, seem almost a decent man. Steiner, as already noted, reinvented Jacob Grill—"son of a rabbi, from Poland"—as Hitler's ideological mentor and projected Hitler himself as something of a Torah-inspired visionary. In a recent film, *Zelig,* Woody Allen uses a fake Oswald Pohl, the head of the SS Economic-Administrative Main Office and, as such, the person chiefly responsible for the concentration camp business, to comment in pseudohistorical terms on a fictitious character that Pohl allegedly "knew" in Nazi Germany. As in every one of these instances, it is a characteristic of the new narrative modes that distinctions between what is real and what is imagined drop away: historical figures take on fictional dimensions, fictional characters are placed within historical settings, and there is an intermingling of illusion and historically accredited reality. These conjunctions of fact and fiction are manifest in a wide body of contemporary literature and everywhere raise the same kinds of questions. How much of the "real" Richard Nixon, for instance, are we to call to mind when we meet a "character" named Richard Nixon in Robert Coover's *The Public Burning?* Is the "Henry Kissinger" named by name in Joseph Heller's *Good as Gold* the Henry Kissinger we know from the Washington years, or is he not? How much of the historical Nat Turner survived in William Styron's *The Confessions of Nat Turner* and how much was passed over, made over, fundamentally changed? To what degree can an author play with, reshape, or distort our sense of the past without doing damage to our overall sense of reality? When, as has been the case, critics call *Sophie's Choice* a "brilliant historical novel," are we not approaching a point of epistemological risk, at which our ability to know the difference between historical fiction and fictitious history begins to diminish and, for some, may begin to disappear?

These questions are not new and could be asked as well about works of literature that date back as far as Shakespeare's history plays and the fiction of Scott and Tolstoy, but in recent years they have assumed a greater degree of seriousness and even taken on a certain urgency. They have done so at a time when "reality" itself has become a more extreme and elusive concept, when our ability to represent it within language has been called into question, and when the political will to misrepresent has become blatant and unrestrained. The aesthetic issues that always attend questions of representation take on a new edge when what is being represented is Hitler and Hitlerism, all the more so at a time when the Nazi Holocaust of the Jews is regularly labeled a "hoax" by the revisionists and their allies and when the image of Hitler is undergoing the kinds of transformation described throughout this book.

What one sees today, in fact, is a double transformation of the historical, for not only is Hitler being fictionalized, but so, too, are his victims, and in ways that often substitute and invert the images of the predator and his prey. A willed blurring of distinctions between Nazis and Jews, and, at its most politically pernicious, a willed equation of the two, is detectable not only in the pages of fiction but in the programmatic deceptions of political life. The categories and conventions of imaginative writing—doppelgänger motifs, tropes of transference and substitution, the signs and symbols of historical projection, conjunction, and inversion—are as well known to the professional journalist and the political propagandist as they are to the fiction writer and are today in wide use. One need only pay attention to the character of political discourse at the United Nations and other international forums to realize that "factions," frauds, and other forms of fictitious history are hardly confined to the realm of literature.

The issue became especially acute during the 1982 Israeli–PLO war in Lebanon. What one witnessed then, and can observe still today, was a transposition of the language of the Holocaust onto a situation that in no way resembled it. The Jews were made out to be "Nazis," the Arabs were suddenly portrayed as the new "Jews," Beirut was likened to "the Warsaw Ghetto," and the charge of "genocide" was broadcast around the world. Menachem Begin, Israel's Prime Minister at the time, was "Hitler," his defense minister was "Eichmann," and the two together were said to be planning a "final solution of the Palestinian question" every bit as ruthless and comprehensive in its design as Hitler's *Endlösung*.

Now it is hardly news that political commentary can be as much a lying game as literature, but the steady stream of misinformation, obfuscation, and willful deception in this instance seemed unprecedented. Moreover, the ruse was being performed not only by the professional propagandists directly involved in the fighting—that one expects in warfare—but by a large number of other, seemingly "neutral" observers, who should have had no immediate cause to participate in the elaboration of such a blatant fiction. Why, then, the impulse to "Nazify" the Lebanon war and to convert its combatants into inverted types of the Holocaust?

The license for the release of new fictions is almost always to be found in prior fictions—in this case, the 1975 United Nations resolution that equated Zionism with racism—but the motives for indulging and perpetuating the fictive sense are more deeply psychological and political. By stealing the language of the Holocaust from the Jews and awarding it to the Arabs—in essence, by translating the Palestinians into "Jews" and the real Jews into their would-be assassins—a prior Jewish claim on the conscience of the West can be vitiated and an enormous and unwanted burden of guilt finally be thrown off. The particular cross-cultural larceny at work here, in other words, brings about a fundamental change in political perception and alters the historical character of *two* wars. The Lebanon war becomes the latest phase of a Jewish campaign against the entire Arab nation as total in its fury as Hitler's war against the Jews, and the Nazi Holocaust, whose genocidal character was actual and not metaphorical, is nullified through the transmutation of its historicity into tropes. The particular politics of forgetting that is at work here proceeded not only by "semantic infiltration"—Daniel Patrick Moynihan's useful phrase for the gradually emerging propaganda war against Israel—but, more radically, by semantic transumption and usurpation, which aims to undo the memory of Jewish suffering under the Nazis by transferring the symbols that kept that memory alive to Israel's enemies. The idea is to delegitimize Jewish history and thereby discredit the notion that, as a result of their exceptional suffering, the Jews have any special claim on the world's sympathy.

For his part, Menachem Begin was also caught in a web of tropological thinking, for as his soldiers began to close in on the PLO in Beirut, the Israeli Prime Minister could conceive of the cornered Arafat only in terms of Hitler holed up in his Führerbunker. The Israeli press wondered aloud: Was Begin fighting the PLO in Lebanon or the Nazis in Berlin? Was he exploiting remembrance of the Holocaust as a political instrument, or did he really see every enemy of the Jews as a Hitler, every war a replay of the Holocaust? Whichever way, in the place of actual events there had emerged a typology of implacable evil, which projected the ghost of the Nazi Führer across the battlefields of Beirut. As Israeli writer Amos Oz recently put it, there are times in the Middle East when it seems as if Adolf Hitler is not only alive and well but is on call for active duty by anyone with a grievance or an enemy.

From all one can see, Hitler is not about to be demobilized soon. In politics and in literature—and as they relate to Hitler there is the temptation for the two to merge and become almost one—all the signs indicate a flourishing career ahead. William Gass, one of our most imaginatively resourceful writers, is at work on a novel that invokes Hitler to explore what he calls a "fascism of the heart." The pornographers will continue to appeal to their own version of this fascination (a fascism of the loins?) by turning out formulaic fiction that links eroticism with Nazism. For those with a voyeur's taste for such things, there will soon be a film version of *The White Hotel,* which, one imagines, will offer movie-goers the opportunity to stare in open-mouthed wonder at the nude bodies lying about Babi Yar. No doubt there will be television replays of "Holocaust," "The Last Days of Hitler," "The Winds of War," "The Bunker," "Blood and Honor," the Speer memoirs—all of which succeed in keeping images of the Third Reich steadily before the viewing public. *The National Lampoon* will recycle more of its Hitler jokes, the *National Examiner* will report sensational new sightings of fugitive Nazis, the revisionists will announce new "evidence" that the Holocaust never happened.

It is predictable that a rock group will emerge that will outdo all others in raucous exhibitionism of Nazi sentiment and paraphernalia and that new New-Style boutiques will highlight Storm-Trooper uniforms for men and something equally brutal for women as the latest craze in fashion. As of this writing, the newest and raciest clothing item in London's Petticoat Lane are Hitler T-shirts, which feature a picture of the Führer under the heading "European Tour 1939–1945." The "tour" commences with "September 1939—Poland" and concludes with "July 1945—Berlin Bunker." For a change-off, one can also pick up black T-shirts at the stalls emblazoned with the word "Bundeswehr."

For years hobby shops have registered steady sales in model replicas of World War II German tanks and planes—cheaper ones for the children, more expensive ones for their elders. As part of this same market, but on a more serious and higher-priced level, there will continue to be a brisk collector's trade in original Nazi insignia, swords, and other symbols of the Reich, as there will be in oversized picture books on World War II weapons and warfare. Richly illustrated "lives" of Hitler will appear, as will expensive, coffee-table albums of concentration camp photographs and artwork. Someone will turn up long-lost Hitler watercolors, medical records, astrological charts, automobiles—anything that Hitler may have touched or been touched by. Our sense of the "family side" of the man will be teased by new revelations about Eva Braun, Blondi, a "mystery woman," a "lost son." Konrad Kujau, the enterprising West German forger, has already announced from jail that when he gets out he will produce before the world a sensation far more dramatic than his now-discredited Hitler diaries—namely, Hitler's daughter. The fact that there never was such a daughter really does not matter, for when it comes to keeping Hitler alive and before the public's hungry eye for news, frauds and fictions serve as well as facts. The crucial point—crucial for being self-perpetuating, inexhaustible, and endlessly marketable—is simply to maintain "the Third Reich, in the person of its Führer, Adolf Hitler, [as] the greatest plot device the world has ever known." What is at stake here, then, is not historical credibility but narrativity—stories, emblems, and images that will fascinate and compel.

True, much of what has just been described is in the realm of kitsch and quatsch—the detritus of history refashioned into cheap and unworthy artifice—but it was at least partly on the rivers of such junk that Hitler originally floated into power and remains afloat still today. It is not high scholarship or high art, let alone high ideals, that sustains him but something a good deal further down in consciousness and culture. Call it the blood lusts of primitive instinct or the anarchic and nihilistic impulses that want to be satisfied free of all restraints. Or call it, as Hitler himself called it, the mad ambition of "Weltmacht oder Niedergang"—"world power or ruin." Whatever else he may exemplify, Hitler stands for, appeals to, and calls forth an unprecedented extremity of destructive will. Charles Hamilton, the New York autograph dealer, probably summed up as well as anyone the secret of Hitler's posthumous appeal when, in considering the value of an object alleged to be Hitler's skull, he said simply, "Hitler is the supreme criminal of all times. He out-Neroes Nero, he out-Caligulas Caligula. Therefore, he is a most fascinating man."

It is easy to exploit a figure that generates such fascination, far less easy to contain the damage it may do once it is released into the world. The fate of symbols is always unpredictable, all the more so when they have behind them as much turbulence and unmastered energy as those that attach to Hitler. One recalls in this context an insight of Elias Canetti, whose notebook jottings of 1942 include the following entry: "Some sentences release their poison only years after." Whether Canetti had been listening to one of Hitler's speeches when he wrote these words is unknown, but one readily sees how they could apply to the rhetoric of the Third Reich and how they might apply as well today, when the words and images of that era have assumed such popular currency. To be sure, they circulate now in another mood and in a different, less dangerous political climate. All the same, there is inherent in the image of Nazism a venom that, once released onto the page and into the mind, has the potential to turn lethal. As imaginative life domesticates images of Hitler and political life continues to exploit him, one should not be surprised to see the old poison once more begin to flow free.

Just where it will go and what damage it may do is anybody's guess. Most of those involved in popularizing Hitler are probably too busy making money and having fun to give any thought to the social and political consequences of their efforts. As for the others, who deliberately set about manipulating historical symbols, the consequences have no doubt been far more precisely calculated by them. In both cases, the appeal to the Third Reich, whether for reasons of commercial or political profit, means a perpetuation in image of the very worst that history has given us and a revivification of the prospect that it may come round once again.

One would rather be rid of the Nazi nightmare once and for all, but it has become too deeply embedded in fantasy life to be quickly or easily denied. The extensions, distortions, and various exploitations of Nazi symbolism have by now become part of the history of the Nazi era as it has penetrated contemporary consciousness. In this respect, Hitler has won, for he knew better than most that if truth has its appeal, so, too, do certain lies, which are every bit as irrepressible once they catch hold. How they have come to catch hold should by now be clear. For years the image of the man and his times has been broadly and successfully projected through the work of novelists, filmmakers, and other fictioneers, and it is they who have assumed and directed the narrative destiny of the Nazi period. Consequently, set loose by a hundred different stories, legends, and myths, the ghost of Hitler now roams through the popular mind in all the shapes that artifice and forgetfulness have combined to give him.

He will not go away soon. As fact, the "Thousand Year Reich" lasted little more than a decade, but as fiction it goes on and on. In the words of Horst Krüger, whose memoir of growing up in Nazi Germany is as prescient as any we have, this Hitler "has played a trick on us," "this Hitler remains with us—all the days of our lives."

BIBLIOGRAPHY

The bibliography lists works referred to in the text as well as related literature read as background material. It is not intended to be comprehensive of the literature on Hitler and Nazism. Since the phenomenon under review here is a popular one, I have included a number of titles in their paperback editions, the form in which most readers are likely to discover them.

Allhoff, Fred. *Lightning in the Night.* Englewood Cliffs, N.J.: Prentice-Hall, 1979.

Améry, Jean. *Radical Humanism.* Trans. Sidney Rosenfeld and Stella Rosenfeld. Bloomington: Indiana University Press, 1984.

Anatoli, A. [Kuznetsov]. *Babi Yar.* Trans. David Floyd. New York: Pocket Books, 1977.

Antrobus, John. *"Hitler in Liverpool" and Other Plays.* London: John Calder, 1983.

Bainbridge, Beryl. *Young Adolf.* New York: George Braziller, 1979.

Barraclough, Geoffrey. "Goodbye, Hitler," *New York Review of Books* (November 19, 1981), pp. 14–16.

Bonker, Frances. *The Mad Dictator: A Novel of Adolf Hitler.* Boston: Chapman & Grimes, 1950.

Boulle, Pierre. "His Last Battle." In his *Because It Is Absurd.* New York: The Vanguard Press, 1971.

Bradbury, Ray. "Darling Adolf." In his *Long After Midnight.* New York: Alfred A. Knopf, 1976.

Brecht, Bertolt. *Der aufhaltsame Aufstieg des Arturo Ui.* Frankfurt: Sukrkamp Verlag, 1965.

Bukowski, Charles. "Swastika." In his *Erections, Ejaculations, Exhibitions and General Tales of Ordinary Madness.* San Francisco: City Lights Books, 1972.

Bullock, Alan. *Hitler, A Study in Tyranny.* New York: Harper & Row, 1964.

Burgess, Anthony. "The Writer among Professors," *Times Literary Supplement* (December 10, 1982), p. 1357.

Cluff, Gladys. "These Good Children." In *Crimes Across the Sea.* Ed. John Creasy and Herbert Brean. New York: Harper & Row, 1964.

Craig, Gordon. *The Germans.* New York: G. P. Putnam's Sons, 1982.

Dahl, Roald. "Genesis and Catastrophe." In his *Tales of the Unexpected.* New York: Vintage Books, 1979.

Dawidowicz, Lucy. *The Jewish Presence: Essays on Identity and History.* New York: Holt, Rinehart and Winston, 1977.

Deighton, Len. *SS-GB.* New York: Ballantine Books, 1979.

Dibner, Martin. *A God for Tomorrow.* New York: Doubleday, 1961.

DiMona, Joseph. *To the Eagle's Nest.* New York: William Morrow & Co., 1980.

Duker, Abraham. "Hitler Meets Haman," *Jewish Spectator* (March 1960), pp. 9–10.

Dundes, Alan, and Thomas Hauschild. "Auschwitz Jokes," *Western Folklore* (October 1983), pp. 249–260.

Ellison, Harlan. "Hitler Painted Roses." In his *New Stories from the Nightside of the World.* New York: Harper & Row, 1978.

Epstein, Leslie. *King of the Jews.* New York: Coward, McCann and Geoghegan, 1979.

Fest, Joachim. *Hitler.* Trans. Richard and Clara Winston. New York: Harcourt, Brace, Jovanovich, 1974.

Field, Allan G. "Pharaoh Meets Hitler," *Jewish Spectator* (April 1945), pp. 15–16.

Fielding, Gabriel. *The Birthday King.* New York: Morrow, 1963.

Fish, Robert L. *Pursuit.* New York: A Berkley Book, 1978.

Forester, C. S. "The Wandering Gentile." In his *The Nightmare.* Los Angeles: Pinnacle Books, 1979.

Frazier, Ian. "The Stuttgart Folders." *The New Yorker* (January 4, 1982), pp. 26–27.

Freeman, Gillian. *Diary of a Nazi Lady.* New York: Ace Books, 1979.

Friedländer, Saul. *Reflections of Nazism: An Essay on Kitsch and Death.* New York: Harper & Row, 1984.

———. *When Memory Comes.* Trans. Helen R. Lane. New York: Farrar, Straus, Giroux, 1979.

Gass, William. "The Tunnel," *Salmagundi* (Winter 1982), pp. 3–60.

Gold, Herbert. *My Last Two Thousand Years.* New York: Random House, 1972.

Goss, Gary. *Hitler's Daughter.* Seacaucus, N.J.: Lyle Stuart, n.d.

Grayson, Richard. "With Hitler in New York." In his *With Hitler in New York and Other Stories.* New York: Taplinger Publishing Co., 1979.

Gronowicz, Antoni. *Hitler's Wife.* Trans. Donald S. Rockwell. New York: Paramount Pub. Co., 1942.

Haffner, Sebastian. *The Meaning of Hitler.* Trans. Ewald Owens. New York: Macmillan, 1979.

Heidemann, Gerd, Leo Pesch, and Thomas Walde. "Hitlers Tagebücher: Der Fall Hess." *Stern* (May 5, 1983), pp. 20–53.

Higgins, Jack. *The Eagle Has Landed.* New York: Holt, Rinehart and Winston, 1975.

"The Hitler Business," *Life* (July 1983), pp. 83–88.

"Hitler Is Alive," *National Police Gazette* (January 1977), pp. 3–49.

"Hitler's Secret Diaries," *Newsweek* (May 2, 1983), pp. 50–60.

Household, Geoffrey. *Rogue Male.* Boston: Little, Brown, 1939.

Bibliography

Hughes, Richard. *The Fox in the Attic.* New York: Harper & Brothers, 1961.
————. *The Wooden Shepherdess.* New York: Harper & Row, 1973.
Hugo, Richard. *The Hitler Diaries.* New York: William Morrow & Company, 1982.
Hulme, George. *The Life and Death of Adolf Hitler.* Toronto: Macmillan of Canada, 1976.

Jones, R. Page. *The Man Who Killed Hitler.* New York: A Jove Book, 1980.

Kardel [Hennecke]. *Adolf Hitler—Begründer Israels.* Geneva: Marva, 1974.
Kempowski, Walter. *Did You Ever See Hitler?* Trans. Michael Roloff. New York: Avon, 1975.
Kermode, Frank. *The Sense of an Ending.* New York: Oxford University Press, 1967.
Kirst, Hans Hellmut. *The Night of the Generals.* Trans. J. Maxwell Brownjohn. New York: Bantam Books, 1965.
————. *The Nights of the Long Knives.* Trans. J. Maxwell Brownjohn. Greenwich, Conn.: Fawcett Crest Book, 1976.
————. *Soldiers' Revolt.* Trans. J. Maxwell Brownjohn. New York: Harper & Row, 1966.
Klein, A. M. *The Hitleriad.* New York: New Directions, 1944.
Kosinski, Jerry. *The Painted Bird,* second edition. Boston: Houghton Mifflin Co., 1976.
Krüger, Horst. *A Crack in the Wall: Growing Up Under Hitler.* Trans. Ruth Hein. New York: Fromm International Publishing Corp., 1982.
Kurtz, Katherine. *Lammas Night.* New York: Ballantine Books, 1983.
Kyle, Duncan. *Black Camelot.* New York: St. Martin's Press, 1978.

Lang, Daniel. *A Backward Look: Germans Remember.* New York: McGraw-Hill, 1979.
Lewis, Wyndham. *Hitler.* London: Chatto & Windus, 1931.
————. *The Hitler Cult.* London: Dent, 1939.
————. *The Jews: Are They Human?* London: George Allen & Unwin, 1939.
Levin, Ira. *The Boys from Brazil.* New York: Random House, 1976.
Liddy, G. Gordon. *Will.* New York: St. Martin's Press, 1980.
Lieberman, Herbert. *The Climate of Hell.* New York: Simon and Schuster, 1978.
Litvinoff, Emanuel. *Falls the Shadow.* New York: Stein and Day, 1983.
Ludlum, Robert. *The Holcroft Covenant.* New York: Bantam Books, 1978.

McCall, Bruce. "The Hitler Formula: Out of the Ashes of World War II and onto the Best Seller List in 14 Easy Steps," *Esquire* (April 1980), pp. 101–102.
McCarthy, Mary. "The Hue and Cry." In her *The Writing on the Wall and Other Literary Essays.* New York: Harcourt, Brace & World, 1970.
McKale, Donald W. *Hitler: The Survival Myth.* New York: Stein and Day, 1981.
MacNamara, Paul. "The Man from Liberty Street." In *Famous Short Stories.* Ed. Kurt Singer. Minneapolis: T. S. Denison & Co., 1968.
Mann, Thomas. "A Brother." In his *Order of the Day: Political Essays and*

Speeches of Two Decades. Trans. H. T. Lowe-Porter. New York: Alfred A. Knopf, 1942.

Marion, James. *The Asgard Solution.* New York: Avon, 1983.

Marlowe, Stephen. *The Valkyrie Encounter.* New York: A Jove/HBJ Book, 1978.

Maser, Werner. *Hitler: Legend, Myth, & Reality.* Trans. Peter and Betty Ross. New York: Harper & Row, 1973.

Mullally, Frederic. *Hitler Has Won.* New York: Simon and Schuster, 1975.

Nietzsche, Friedrich. "The Use and Abuse of History." In his *Complete Works.* Ed. Oscar Levy. Vol. V. Trans. Adrian Collins. London: George Allen & Unwin, Ltd., 1909.

Noyes, Alfred. *If Judgment Comes.* New York: Frederick A. Stokes, 1941.

Patterson, Harry. *To Catch a King.* New York: Stein and Day, 1979.

Pelz, Werner and Lotte. *I Am Adolf Hitler.* Richmond, Va.: John Knox Press, 1971.

Puccetti, Roland. *The Death of the Führer.* New York: St. Martin's Press, 1972.

Radin, Max. *The Day of Reckoning.* New York: Alfred A. Knopf, 1943.

Reed, Douglas. *Downfall.* London: Jonathan Cape, 1942.

Reuter, Florizel von. *Twilight of the Gods.* New York: Cultural Press, 1962.

Rjndt, Philipe van. *The Trial of Adolf Hitler.* New York: Summit Books, 1978.

Rose, Richard. *The Wolf.* New York: Zebra Books, 1980.

Roth, Philip. *The Ghost Writer.* New York: Farrar, Straus & Giroux, 1979.

Shaw, George Bernard. *Geneva.* Collected in *Geneva, Cymbeline Refinished, & Good King Charles.* London: Constable and Company, 1946.

Singer, Isaac Bashevis. *Enemies, A Love Story.* New York: Farrar, Straus & Giroux, 1972.

Sissini [Chorafas, Dimitris N.]. *Samuel Hitler.* Darmstadt, West Germany: Melzer Verlag, 1973.

Snodgrass, William. *The Führer Bunker: A Cycle of Poems in Progress.* Brockport, N.Y.: Boa Editions, 1977.

Spinrad, Norman. *The Iron Dream.* New York: Avon, 1972.

Spiraux, Alain. *Time Out.* Trans. Frances Keene. New York: Times Books, 1978.

Steiner, George. *The Portage to San Cristóbal of A.H.* New York: Simon and Schuster, 1981.

Stiller, Klaus. *H.: Protokoll.* Neuwied: Hermann Luchterhand Verlag, 1970.

Styron, William. *Sophie's Choice.* New York: Random House, 1979.

Syberberg, Hans-Jürgen. *Hitler, A Film from Germany.* Trans. Joachim Neugroschel. New York: Farrar, Straus & Giroux, 1982.

Teufels, Drake. "The Real Adolf Hitler." In *Book of Books.* Ed. Jeff Greenfield. New York: National Lampoon, Inc., 1979.

Thomas, D. M. *The White Hotel.* New York: Viking, 1981.

Toland, John. *Adolf Hitler.* Garden City: Doubleday & Co., 1976.

Trevor-Roper, Hugh. "Hitler: A Catalogue of Errors," *The Times* (May 14, 1983), p. 8.

Bibliography

————. *The Last Days of Hitler.* 3rd ed. New York: Macmillan, 1965.

————. "Secrets that Survived the Bunker," *The Times* (April 23, 1983), p. 8.

Turner, John. "Adolf Hitler Is Alive," *National Examiner* (July 6, 1982), pp. 2–3.

Unger, Michael, ed. *The Memoirs of Bridget Hitler.* London: Duckworth, 1979.

"The Uses of History in Fiction," *The Southern Literary Journal*, (Spring 1969), pp. 57–90 [a panel discussion with Ralph Ellison, William Styron, R. P. Warren, and C. Vann Woodward].

Wager, Walter. *Time of Reckoning.* New York: Playboy Press, 1977.

Waite, Robert G. L. *The Psychopathic God: Adolf Hitler.* New York: Basic Books, 1977.

Weill, Gus. *The Führer Seed.* New York: William Morrow, 1979.

Weiss, Ernst. *The Eyewitness.* Trans. Ella R. W. McKee. Boston: Houghton Mifflin Company, 1977.

Werth, German. "*Was wäre geschehen, wenn—?*" *Stuttgarter Zeitung* (March 6, 1982).

"Wie Sternreporter Gerd Heidemann die Tagebücher fand," *Stern* (April 28, 1983), pp. 20–37.

Wiesel, Elie. "Myth and History." In *Myth, Symbol, and Reality.* Ed. Alan Olson. South Bend, Ind.: University of Notre Dame Press (1980), pp. 20–30.

"Das Wind-Ei: Wie die Blamage mit den Hitler 'Tagebüchern' zustande kam," *Stern* (May 19, 1983), pp. 20–30.

Young, Michael. *The Trial of Adolf Hitler.* New York: E. P. Dutton, 1944.

INDEX

Index

Index